DEVELOPMENT FINANCE

DEVELOPMENT FINANCE
PLANNING AND CONTROL

Ursula K. Hicks

1965

OXFORD UNIVERSITY PRESS

NEW YORK AND OXFORD

© Oxford University Press 1965

PRINTED IN THE UNITED STATES OF AMERICA

PREFACE

SOME eight years ago Sir Arthur Lewis made the point that although much had been written about the economics of development, very little indeed had been said about the all important problem of its financing. Since that time much thought and energy has gone into advising the developing countries as to the fiscal and financial measures they should take to support the process. This advice has been given through Commissions, Conferences, Workshops and Seminars in bewildering multiplicity, and also through lectures and courses provided in the universities. But it still remains true that there is no book which deals simply and systematically with the various fiscal and financial aspects of development. The need for one is now considerably more urgent than it was in 1956.

I have written this book in an endeavour to meet this need, and as an answer to the repeated requests of teachers and students to tell them what to read. My object has been to set out the basic principles of expenditure choice, monetary and fiscal measures, and budgetary control, as simply as possible, clothing them in a practical dress so that they can be of direct assistance to planners and administrators.

I think that I have done my share of advising: from a consultancy assignment to the U.N. in India and to the Revenue Allocation Commission in Nigeria in 1950, on a two-man Commission with my husband in Jamaica in 1954, and on a Central Bank Assignment in Ceylon in 1957. More recently I have been Fiscal Commissioner in Uganda and in the Caribbean (both in 1962), and Adviser to the Government of Eastern Nigeria in 1964. In addition, there have been Consultancy Missions and visits to many other countries, in Asia, Africa, and Latin America.

These various experiences form one source of what I have here set down; the other main source is the course of lectures which I have given annually in the University of Oxford on 'Financial Problems of Emergent Countries'. It has been a particular pleasure to renew acquaintances with successive generations of students of this course when I have subsequently visited their countries. It is my hope that they and their Ministers will find in my book some recompense for all that they have done to improve my understanding of their problems.

Ursula K. Hicks,
Oxford, November 1964

Addendum to Preface

Since the completion of this book the British Budget legislation of 1965 withdraws the Overseas Trading Corporation concession (see p. 98). In addition to this direct hindrance to investment in development countries, indirect disincentives may well arise through the fact that the income taxes on companies in these countries are at present generally higher than the corporation tax to which alone companies in the U.K. will be subject.

U. K. Hicks.

LIST OF CONTENTS

LIST OF TABLES

DEVELOPMENT FINANCE

CHAPTER ONE

STRATEGY FOR DEVELOPMENT: THE IMPACT OF FINANCE

1. *Financial Aspects of Planning*

IN this book I am concerned with the economic development of the poorer countries of the world, countries which we all agree have a special need of advice and assistance. I propose to call them 'development countries' (in preference to 'underdeveloped' or 'developing') in order to emphasise that they are undergoing a particular process, watched and fostered by the U.N. and other international agencies, as well as by the advanced countries. By 'economic development' I simply mean growth in real income per head, while not losing sight of the fact that an increase in the gross national product is unacceptable unless it also implies some betterment of the lot of the mass of the people. Economic development has a social and redistributional as well as an economic aspect.

Many of the problems that have to be faced in drawing up a development programme are similar in kind, irrespective of the type of country and its constitution: unitary or federal, authoritarian or parliamentarian, or of various degrees in between. I shall however be almost wholly concerned with 'mixed' economies, where some responsibility is left to private enterprise not only in agriculture (as is almost universal), but also in industry and commerce.

In a development country public finance and the development process impinge on each other at every turn. The development programme determines what types of expenditure will need to be adopted in the public sector and to be encouraged in the private sector. This in turn determines what fiscal policy will be required; while the degree of development attained determines very largely what taxes it is feasible to levy.

In the development countries the process of improvement consists mainly in the application of well established techniques to imperfectly known conditions: climates whose vagaries have not been adequately recorded, minerals that have been only partly discovered or proved, populations whose precise size and growth rates are uncertain. While original research leading to the invention and application of new techniques is not ruled out (and should certainly be encouraged)[1] a tremendous amount of thought and effort is required merely to adapt techniques already worked out in the advanced countries to the very different circumstances in which they will be required to function.[2] This process of adaptation is essential to the success of the development programme. Unless it is properly carried out there is likely to be much waste of funds and material, disappointment, and frustration.

The process of development is inevitably very costly, so that it is just as important to have a good financial plan, making optimal use of financial resources, as it is to have a good economic plan, making optimal use of the real resources available. What the nature of a good financial plan will be turns very largely on two factors; first the character of the country and its particular economic potentialities, and secondly the degree of development already attained when the development exercise starts. For instance some countries, such as British Guiana, Sierra Leone, and Afghanistan, possess important minerals, but to make them readily available requires a great deal of heavy investment; while other places (such as tea areas in Uganda) can be developed with relatively little investment apart from roads. In view of these factors it will be useful to glance briefly at those common characteristics of the development countries that are relevant in shaping their development plans. It is on these that their financial plans and possibilities mainly turn.

Every development country poses problems peculiar to itself that require individual consideration in the light of its physical features, natural resources, the size and sophistication of its people, and their initial wealth.[3] On the other hand there are a substantial

1. For instance research into tropical diseases, on which important work is being done in African teaching hospitals and Research Institutes. With rapid air communication this has become a matter of importance to the advanced countries also.

2. It is unnecessary to elaborate this point. Development countries are strewn with imported equipment which has proved a misfit for the work it has to do. The causes may be such things as physical or climatic differences, the small amount of product to be processed, the narrow range of the market to be served. Again imported equipment may be too complicated for the type of labour available.

3. I was much impressed with this factor in development when, as Fiscal Commissioner in 1962, I visited in turn the British Caribbean Islands. Even small islands, possibly within sight of each other, exhibit striking differences in soil, climate, elevation and in the origins and traditions of their people. Their

number of common characteristics that we can expect to find, in a greater or less degree, in almost any of them. In addition we can trace broad regional affinities—in Asia and the Far East, in Africa, and in Latin America, and elsewhere—that provide further common ground on which to build.

2. Development Countries: The Poor and The Very Poor

The most universal characteristics of development countries (as is well recognised) is their poverty and consequential low standard of living. But it is necessary to draw a sharp line (particularly on grounds of revenue possibilities) between the very poor countries, with per capita incomes not above £35 per annum (and in some cases actually under £20), and the not so poor countries, with per capita incomes ranging somewhere between £80 and £150. In view of the paucity of reliable national income and population statistics nothing very precise can be stated, but it is safe to say (for instance) that India, Pakistan and several other South East Asian countries, as well as most of the East, West and Central African states, fall into the first class. In the more wealthy class come Malaya, most of the West Indies, and certainly the better off of the Latin American countries (but their statistics are singularly unreliable). Naturally not all countries fit neatly into these two categories. For instance Ghana and Ceylon are distinctly better off than their neighbours. But these exceptions do not diminish the importance of making the distinction between the two groups.

Even the wealthiest of the development countries is very poor compared with the advanced countries, although not necessarily with some of the European Mediterranean countries, which in some ways—and parts—have a right to be treated as development countries also.[1] I am not concerned to argue here whether the gap between the rich countries as a whole and the poor countries as a whole is growing wider or narrower; but it is undoubtedly true that some of the poorer countries are growing faster than others, so there are certainly some gaps that are widening.

economic potentialities have as a consequence to be individually assessed. cf. Report of Fiscal Commission for Eastern Caribbean Cmd 1991 of 1963 and Report of Economic Commission. 'A Survey of Economic Potential and Capital Needs of the Leeward Islands, Windward Islands and Barbados' by C. O'Loughlin and H. O'Neale. HMSO 1963.

1. Italy thus treats her Southern Provinces, including Sicily and Sardinia.

The wealth differences between countries are estimated in terms of cash incomes; but in the very poor countries especially this is apt to be misleading, owing to the presence of 'subsistence' sectors where the population produces practically all that it consumes and has very little contact with the money economy of the rest of the world. Conceptual as well as practical difficulties hinder the estimation of the true per capita income in these countries, and it may well be that the poverty of these countries is exaggerated by the statistics; but it is serious enough in any case.[1]

Apart from anything else, the presence of a subsistence sector implies that there is likely to be much more difference between rich and poor than in an advanced country, even before allowance is made for redistributive public expenditure and taxation in the latter. This fact seems to be well authenticated in the statistics.[2] In the early stages of development this income dispersion appears to grow rather than to diminish (for reasons that we shall examine in a minute); but the nature and significance of income differences tend to change over time. Before development has caught hold, the rich tend to be either some type of traditional ruler or else religious communities. Neither the wealth nor the incomes of these sectors are easily drawn into the development process, either spontaneously or through taxation. Rulers and other wealthy citizens tend to spend heavily on consumption and on the maintenance of large households of more or less unemployed dependants; religious communities are often mainly interested in beautifying their sacred buildings. Both groups may include large landowners, but they are unlikely to farm their property in a way that contributes to the gross national product (G.N.P.). Their territorial influence, however, may enable them to exert great political influence. This phenomenon is apparent in such diverse economies as Northern Nigeria, Pakistan, Ceylon, and some parts of Latin America.

As development progresses the importance of the original élite tends to decline; but they are more than replaced by the new rich. In many young democracies some of the most conspicuous consumption is that indulged in by Ministers. This not only wastes the taxpayer's money, but if carried to excess may cause severe social and political unrest. In India this phenomenon is less

---

1. For further discussion of this point see below, p. 135.
2. cf. for instance S. Kuznets, 'Income Growth and Income Inequality', *American Economic Review*, 1955.

prevalent, at least at the Union level (thanks in no small degree to the continued influence of the Ghandian philosophy of poverty and service). In India, on the other hand, a second element among the new rich has emerged with great prominence: the business tycoon, in manufacturing and commerce. It is only a matter of time before he also makes his presence felt in Africa. These new élite clearly have liquid resources available for taxation in a way the old élite did not; but they tend to be adept at avoidance and evasion. In the Indian case there is the further danger of possible disincentive effects of high taxation on a class which, whatever its faults, is vital for development. We shall have at a later stage to discuss this aspect of fiscal policy in detail.

In all this there is ample explanation of the failure of the gap between rich and poor to narrow. Lower down the income scale, however, further changes are taking place. In economies where any sort of skill is rare and where the bulk of the population is accustomed only to rural conditions, successful urban factory workers quickly establish themselves as a middle range élite. Organised in powerful trade unions they may achieve a quasi-monopoly position, living at a very much higher standard than the rural population.[1] Even if there are not powerful trade unions this situation may easily lead to the development of what has been described as a 'dual economy', with a deep cleavage developing between urban and rural living conditions in general, although, owing to immigration, the worst poverty is still often to be found in the towns. Conspicuous examples of this phenomenon are to be found in Italy and Japan, which in many respects are highly developed countries. It is also prevalent over much of Latin America and is of increasing importance in India. A related phenomenon in many of these countries is the cleavage between large and small scale industry, the former highly efficient and profitable, the latter often old-fashioned and inefficient. In countries with a severe population problem governments tend, however, to support the small scale and inefficient industry, for the reason that it is usually a big employer of labour, even if this policy is not in the best interest of development. As we shall have many occasions to observe, these stresses and strains of development greatly complicate the problem of a rational economic programme and its finance.

1. In almost all the Caribbean Islands, the Chief Minister is also the chief trade union leader.

3. Population Explosion and Immobilities

Uneven development of any of the types just discussed is closely related to two characteristic phenomena of development countries: population pressure and unequal natural endowment between different parts of the country. These factors are themselves inter-related, since population pressure tends to be more serious in the poor areas, both because of the poverty of resources and frequently because the birth rate is higher. Thanks to recent improvements in tropical medicine[1] it is now not uncommon in the development countries to find death rates as low as or lower than in the most advanced. Although this can only be a temporary phenomenon until the expectation of life catches up with that of the advanced countries, in the meantime the expansion of the working age groups on the one side and the fall in infant mortality on the other not only imply a rapid rate of population increase, but pose special problems in the field of public expenditure, as we shall see. Those countries where population was already large in relation to available resources before serious development started (such as India, Egypt, some of the West Indian Islands, and, one should add, Japan) are already experiencing a population explosion. Of all such countries only Japan has so far taken serious steps to get the problem in hand, although effective methods of family planning can now be made available (although with some difficulty), at reasonable prices. In the remaining development countries there is still time to prevent a complete explosion if the right steps are taken; but even so many new economic opportunities must be provided if serious unemployment is to be avoided.

One result of the continuance of backward sectors and areas in development countries is that for a considerable time the development process fails to break down traditional socio-economic rigidities and immobilities. The persistence of these in turn reacts on the rate of attainable progress. It is not uncommon to find that development makes quite a good start, but then seems to slacken off, having come up against a blank wall of inertia. The long run solution to this state of affairs must be better education and better communications; but these items are only a part of the public expenditure strategy which needs to be adopted. A tax policy that

---

1. Of which by far the most important has been the conquest of malaria by D.D.T. spraying.

reaches down into the villages can also make a useful contribution and can have a quicker reaction. But care must be taken to see that too much is not attempted too quickly. High tax rates which can only be partially enforced inculcate bad habits of evasion, and in the case of those on whom they can be enforced may lead to real hardship. They are, however, a considerable temptation to inexperienced administrations.

It must be faced that the development countries are backward mainly because their resources are poor or at least not readily accessible. To raise their standard of life consequently implies an additional struggle beyond what many of the advanced countries have ever had to face. The first necessity in most of them is to raise agricultural productivity. Generally speaking, the agricultural sector is still the largest, so that on this ground alone it merits special attention, whether we have in mind an expansion of export crops (the soundest way to improve the balance of payments in the short run), or an expansion of food crops for the home population, who, as they rise in the world and undertake harder work, will both want, and need, to eat more. But here these countries are up against serious difficulties of climate and rainfall.

High temperatures, alternation of monsoon and drought, and perpetual equal days and nights are factors inimical to growing a wide range of crops. Most development countries suffer from one or more of these limitations. It is not surprising that the range of tropical crops is much narrower than that of temperate zone crops, and competition is consequently more severe. There is no doubt, however, that with more research and experiment very great increases in productivity can be achieved, both in the output of particular crops and in the range of production that can be undertaken in particular countries.

4. *The Impact of Independence*

So far the common characteristics of development countries that we have discussed have all been related to natural phenomena. On the whole they are not favourable to rapid improvement; but fortunately a number of development countries have other resources, such as valuable minerals or tourist opportunities, that enable them to expand more rapidly. A difficult set of problems is presented to many of them by the fact that they have only recently gained their independence. This is of course a most exhilarating experience, but it is at the same time very disturbing. It is almost universal to find that the glories of independence day, the high hopes and the high spending that accompany it, are quickly followed by post-independence depression, or at least stagnation and balance of payments difficulties.

Moreover, independence gives rise to many additional costs. An independent country is a citizen of the world. It must pay fairly lavishly for overseas representation in the leading centres. Its Ministers and their staffs must make frequent journeys to meetings of world organisations. It probably will have to spend a large part of its budget on defence, which was previously looked after by the metropolitan country. All these commitments occur at a time when it is only too likely that the administration will be disrupted by the sudden departure of experienced expatriate officers and there has been no time to train local officers to take their place. A development country is lucky if it even has a cadre of educated citizens on which to draw. In India, exceptionally, where the steps to independence were spread over more than twenty years, there was already established an administrative service of high calibre. Yet India found itself under great strain to cover the needs of the newly absorbed Native States, quite apart from those of defence.

Elsewhere, as the steps to independence became more and more telescoped, the situation was inevitably much more serious, sometimes reaching the point of complete breakdown and everywhere leading to a serious deterioration in the calibre and reliability of the administration. On the political front, many development countries started their independent life with new institutions, including for first time adult suffrage and a Ministerial system. In spite of strenuous efforts on the part of retiring expatriate officers, neither Ministers nor voters understood their responsibilities properly. In very many countries Ministers were much more interested in promoting the activities of their own Ministries than in furthering the interests of the nation. Individual and often contradictory policies made an adequate control of public expenditure impossible. It thus fell to the civil service to pull things together and to educate Ministers in their proper role, and as we have seen the civil service was itself severely weakened by the impact of independence. In these circumstances it was inevitable that standards of administration should sag, especially in the unpleasant tasks of the assessment and collection of taxes. It was also inevitable that government should cost a good deal more than it had done under colonial administration.[1]

The conditions just described have been largely unavoidable in view of the suddenness with which independence has been gained, particularly in Africa. There is no compelling reason why they should be other than transitional; but to get round them calls for a constructive and confident policy on the part of the new governments, combined with all the support and training that can be made available by the advanced countries.

There is, however, one more point to make in this connection. To start with, the public sectors in development countries tend to be too small to act as effective regulators or growth stimulators. It is common to find that tax revenue as a percentage of the G.N.P. is of the order of about 12 per cent, sometimes even lower, as compared with 30 per cent or above in the advanced countries. In the advanced countries governments can to a considerable extent control the level of economic activity by adjusting their tax and expenditure policy. They can also back up fiscal policy by monetary measures. In the development countries this is not possible because financial institutions are not developed. If the banking habit is not general, credit policy must necessarily be ineffective. Moreover, many development countries have only recently left the shelter of the simple (even if rigid) Currency Board system to venture out on the sea of central banking. Those that had central banks established at an earlier stage are finding that they follow too closely the model of those in the advanced countries, which were never intended as instruments of growth. We shall have to examine these matters in Chapter 3.

5. *Regional Affinities*

The characteristics of development countries so far discussed may be said to be common to them all in greater or less degree. We must now take a glance at the regional affinities of those situated in the major areas of the world: South and South East Asia, Africa, and Latin America. There is increasing evidence of a

---

1. Even in the absence of independence the expansion of government activities into economic fields implied that the costs of government were bound to rise. Even before he was swept away by the tide of political change the all-purpose District Officer had ceased to be able to cover the requirements of government.

growth in awareness among them of common regional interests. This movement is paralleled by a growing emphasis on common regional interests among the advanced countries, as in continental Europe. This new awareness is very largely a result of growing ease and speed of communications. Its roots, however, lie much deeper, in a realisation of common political and economic interests, as well as common ethnic, social and religious affinities.

The desire for drawing together into larger groups among the development countries springs from a number of motives. Politically it is prompted by a wish to play an important part in world counsels. (In this aspect it is related to the demand for complete independence by very small countries that are clearly not economically viable.) So far, none of these groups has attained any sort of stable political integration since gaining independence, but this may come at any time. On the ethnic side there is a close relationship (for instance) between the African states, and again in South East Asia between Thailand, Burma, and the successor states to French Indo-China. On the religious and social side there is a close affinity among these Buddhist states, or among the Muslim states of the Middle East, or the Catholic states of Latin America. Sometimes supporting but sometimes cutting across these affinities are the bonds created by a common inheritance of legal and administrative traditions from former colonial powers. Thus (for instance) local administrators from India and Pakistan, from Nigeria and Malaya, all 'speak the same language' in far more senses than the purely linguistic one. When they come together they understand each others' institutions almost as well as they do their own. The same is no doubt true of the former French colonies in South East Asia and Africa.

To examine these relationships in detail would form a fascinating subject for research, but it is one for sociologists, not for economists. Their relevance for our purpose lies in the way in which they help to mould the pattern of economic growth, the institutions through which it will be implemented, and the tax system through which it will be financed. Moreover, these common traditions can be of very considerable assistance in forwarding the development process. They make it possible, for instance, for countries which are just learning the art of planning to borrow experts from the more experienced development countries, such as India, knowing that they will understand the organisation and the tax system through which they will have to work. Increasingly this help given by one development country to others will be of far more relevance in many ways than the advice the advanced countries can give. The growing awareness of regional affinities among the development countries is fostered by the U.N. Regional organisations E.C.A.F.E., E.C.L.A., and E.C.A.;[1] and, reciprocally, it is enhancing the importance of the help such bodies as the World Health Organisation, the Food and Agriculture Organisation, and U.N.E.S.C.O. can give. Increasingly these organisations can view in an informed way the common problems of groups of countries taken together, and country representatives can be brought together in conferences and working parties, where they meet each other and learn much from the similarity of their problems.[2] Through this medium also the services of international experts who are not only of higher calibre than the countries could individually afford, but also have specialised in their particular Region, are made available. Although the U.N. Regions are so large that they inevitably cover a wide range of climatic and other economic differences, within them are many common economic problems, especially on the side of agriculture, where the comparative approach that these experts can bring is particularly useful.

6. *Steps in Development Strategy*

From this brief review of the development countries' problems it will be evident that strategy for development has a great number of facets and can be by no means simple. A point that is sometimes overlooked needs emphasis here. Although a country may only just be starting out on a co-ordinated programme of development, it will already have been provided with a certain amount of public investment in basic services such as communications, education, and public health. Strategy for development thus has two distinct aspects: on' the one hand the maintenance and improvement of existing works and services, on the other the construction of new works and the introduction of new ways of producing goods and services, whether through the improved use of land, the introduction of manufacturers, or the exploitation of mineral resources. There are examples of countries which get so carried away by the

1. The Economic Commissions respectively for Asia, Latin America and Africa.
2. This was illustrated in an expert Conference ('Regional Technical Assistance Seminar' in official terms) on Investment in Education which I attended in Bangkok in April 1964.

excitement and prestige of development that they tend to neglect
the needs of operation, replacement, and maintenance of existing
works; equipment deteriorates, the salaries of civil servants and
teachers fall into arrears. It hardly needs saying that such a course
will lead to serious imbalance, if not to political and social trouble.
It should not be necessary for the central government to bear the
whole responsibility for balanced growth; but it has to bear most
of the costs of providing the physical infrastructure, and it has at
the very least a general responsibility for seeing that development
is making the optimum use of resources for the good of the
economy as a whole.

We can distinguish four steps in the strategy of development
which need separate consideration. First comes a general and preliminary review of priorities, primarily within the government
field, at the individual project level. This in itself is quite a complicated business; in the next chapter we shall have to discuss
criteria of choice in some detail. But no project stands by itself;
each is related to other projects and to existing services. Hence the
second step must be the consideration of these relationships in
order to maximise the benefits accruing from a group of projects
considered together, so that the total benefit will be greater than
the sum of the individual benefits.

This phenomenon, which is sometimes called 'external economies', or more conveniently 'overspill', is of great importance in
planning public expenditure.[1] Overspill does not always work in a
favourable direction; for instance the implementation of one
scheme, or even the further expansion of an existing service, may
reduce the benefits of other projects. There comes a point when the
decision to proceed with one project actually excludes the implementation of another (for instance, alternative dams on the same
river). This danger needs to be watched, but in a development
country the possibilities of favourable overspill are usually much
larger than the chances of unfavourable effects.

When a preliminary programme of eligible projects has been
drawn up, planning must move over from the micro- to the macro-
side, to consider the economy as a whole and the extent to which
the individual elements of the plan are compatible within the range
of economic and financial possibilities. The third and fourth steps

---

1. External economies are also possible on the tax side, as when the information required for one tax assists in the assessment of another, i.e. income tax
and wealth tax.

consequently are concerned with the review of resources available for development expenditure in the light of the resources needed for the operation of existing services and the maintenance of existing works. These resources need to be considered in two aspects; first the availability of physical resources, of land, labour, and equipment; and secondly the financial resources to pay for them.

In the short run it is probable that the most serious bottleneck will be in respect of physical resources (so that reviewing them will constitute the third step). To a limited extent it is possible to make good shortages of labour and equipment by imports. In respect of technical and managerial skills some use will probably have to be made of foreign help in any case. It is, however, very difficult for a development country to import the most suitable types of equipment for its purposes from what is already available in the world. Unavailability of the most appropriate sort of equipment has important repercussions on the choice of techniques. Some projects can be successfully (if not optimally) implemented with a variety of techniques, depending on the resources available. Others demand a particular technique, and if this is not available they had better be demoted to a lower place in the list of priorities.

In contrast to these difficulties concerning the supply of physical resources, in the short period the fourth step, the supply of financial resources, is likely to be relatively easy. There is no country so poor that it cannot quickly raise additional tax revenue if it has the will to do so, most simply by more accurate and thorough assessment and collection of existing taxes. In respect of foreign borrowing also, once a country has adopted a sensible development plan which seems to be within its powers, it will probably have little difficulty in borrowing the balance that cannot be met from home resources. Indeed aid may be proffered to an embarrassing extent, in the sense that to accept it for too large a number of individual projects is to run the risk of financial imbalance and stringency in other parts of the economy. We shall be returning to discuss these problems at greater length in Chapter 3.

In the longer run, however, the relative position of physical and financial resources is likely to be reversed. Gradually more and more of the population can be turned into a useful labour force. As contacts and communications improve they will become eager to better their position. The 'backward sloping' supply curve of labour, about which so much has been written, is compounded of ignorance, lack of opportunity, and probably also substandard physique. These will all be ameliorated as development progresses. Skills, managerial and entrepreneurial capacity will develop within the country. Experience will show which resources are most worth developing and what equipment and techniques are optimum for the purpose. It may well be that these will need to change as development gathers momentum. The first techniques become obsolete, as better methods become practical, just as in an advanced country technical innovation makes older techniques inappropriate. When resources become generally available advance can take place much more rapidly and on a wider front.

On the other hand, after a time, finances are all too likely to develop symptoms of strain, and the balance of payments to experience increasing weakness. Except in the very long run few of the infrastructure works and services contribute directly to the G.N.P. or to tax potential, save in so far as more tax can be extracted from workers employed on construction and those from whom they make purchases. Projects for which it is easy to borrow abroad often require a long construction period even if they are ultimately productive. Nevertheless they are attractive both to borrowers and lenders, to borrowers often partly for prestige reasons, to lenders because they feel there will be something to show. Normally a loan covers only the cost of the project in a very narrow sense, perhaps not even including land and on site costs. It is too often overlooked that this is only the beginning of the government's commitments. Much secondary investment will be required, both on subsidiary works and on the selection and training of co-operating labour, before full advantage can be derived from the new installations. We shall have to discuss this problem in detail later.

There remains the problem of debt service. Especially if this has to be made in a foreign currency there will be a heavy strain on the balance of payments (the true burden of a debt is the high additional taxes that have to be raised to service it). This is the rock on which many earlier developers foundered: the United States, Canada, and Australia were all in trouble more than once. It is true that at that time borrowers had to pay market rates of interest (although on the whole these were lower than they are at present). Nowadays it is common for arrangements to be made for rates of interest well below the market, and for the repayment of principal to be postponed for some years. These arrangements are much to the advantage of borrowers, if they act wisely, that is, if they do not let themselves be carried away and the balance of their plans distorted by what appears to be a good bargain, and if they make adequate provision for service at the end of the period of respite. If these steps are not taken it will be found that almost unawares a heavy debt commitment will have been accumulated; in fact several development countries already find themselves in this predicament. In Chapter 3 we shall be concerned with means for preventing it.

The problems just discussed underline the necessity of looking forward over a period of years in the development programme. Both real and financial resources need to be sufficient to secure the full and continuous operation of services, both old and new. Forward thinking is especially important in respect of salaries and wages. For instance, every new school creates heavy additional commitments in salaries and running costs, while at the same time allowance must also be made for normal pay increments due to the ageing of established teachers (this process is sometimes referred to as 'creep'). In addition demands for higher salaries for teachers and civil servants are a virtual certainty, especially if poor expenditure control has not prevented a rise in local living costs.

Quite distinct, but no less important than period programming, is the annual review of the finances of the economy in the national budget. To be successful these two exercises (the budget and the plan) need to be closely integrated. Neither can safely be given so much priority that it distorts the other. It is unfortunate if the budget review of resources available in the year reveals that plan projects are more than can be managed, and will have to be drastically rephased. It is equally unfortunate if a narrow insistence on plan implementation breaks the budget and the balance of payments, or if the legitimate expectations of private enterprise have to be disappointed because the government has not conducted its affairs wisely.

These matters will be our special concern in Chapters 7 and 8, when we have considered the make-up of the structure of public expenditure and its appropriate finances, matters which will occupy us in Chapters 2–5.

CHAPTER TWO

CHOICE IN THE PUBLIC EXPENDITURE
PROGRAMME

1. Types of Public Expenditure

In the last chapter the need for thinking forward in the development programme was emphasised. The enormous advances which
have been made over the last generation in the theory and practice
of statistics and econometrics now make it possible to quantify
this thinking. So long as the necessary data are made available,
the forward thinking for an economy can be carried out in a
number of ways, depending on the institutions and ideology of the
country. The Plan may be fully comprehensive and obligatory on
the whole economy, as in the Soviet countries. Or the formal plan
may relate only to the public sector, including nationalised industries and factories (as in India), or it may be extended to the
private sector by discussion persuasion (as in France).[1] Or little
or no attempt may be made to affect the private sector except in
indirect ways (as in the U.K. until recently). In the U.S.A. no
formal public sector plan is made (as we shall see in Chapter 6
this is a considerably more complicated exercise in a federation
than in a unitary country). But American statistics are exceptionally good, and it is expected that the information provided
will be sufficient for sensible planning by private and state
planners.

In fact an increasing number of the advanced countries are
finding it advantageous to make comprehensive forward estimates[2]
of resource allocation, at least in the public sector, covering
periods of three to five years ahead. Such planning is necessarily
in constant prices—both because this is essential for real compari-
sons, and because price movements cannot be foreseen; but a
growth rate for the economy can be included in the calculation.
The great advantage of such forward thinking—and the main
reason why it has been adopted in the U.K.—is that it is necessary

1. For a discussion of French planning, see below, p. 136.
2. cf. the U.K. Public Expenditure in 1967 Cmd 2235 of 1963.

if an accumulation of casual and unrelated expenditure decisions is to be avoided.[1]

Thus the advanced countries can effectively choose how much planning fits their conditions and needs; for development countries it can confidently be asserted that a period plan is a necessary condition of progress. As we have seen, in many development countries progress would be easier if the public sector were to be enlarged, by extending its scope. This can only be achieved in an orderly manner if a summary of desirable expansions and expected resources is drawn up. There are many items of growth, especially in the early stages of development, which can only be looked after by the central government. It is most important that it should be possible to see these in relation to each other and against the background of the whole economy.

The planning of expansion has two aspects: physical (techno-logical) and economic. With the former we are not concerned: but in Chapter 7 we shall be discussing in some detail the economic and management side of the construction and implementation of plans. Here we are concerned with broader issues.

For the purpose of plan summarisation it is necessary to classify public expenditure in some meaningful way. Starting from the basic services of administration and defence, we pass to the physical structure of communications, ports and airfields, to public utilities and other forms of state enterprise, to the improvement of agriculture and the promotion of industry, to the social services, especially education and public health. The now well known group-ing of these into infrastructure (social and economic) and super-structure is useful as a first step, especially as a means of quickly checking balance in the programme; but for more detailed use it leads to certain difficulties.

In the first place it must be recognised that the classification into structures cannot be hard and fast, especially as between social and economic infrastructure or overheads. For instance the balance of education expenditure will not be right unless it is remembered that educational systems are neither purely economic nor purely social. Again, water and electricity supplies (for instance) are used both in production, as economic overheads, and in consumption, for domestic purposes which are mainly social.

Second, and more important, projections tend to be confined)

1. Described by the (Plowden) Committee on the Control of Public Expen-diture (1961) as 'piecemeal commitments'; further discussed below, p. 139.

to development projects, and thus the expansion that is currently occurring in such things as administration and defence tends to go unnoticed. As we have seen, it is inevitable that government should cost more than it used to do, both because governments are expected to do more things and because independence is expensive. Some countries have also inherited a costly structure of civil service salaries designed for expatriates, and these need to be readjusted to the salary structure of the rest of the economy. Even allowing for all this, administrative expenses have risen much more than should have been expected, and now tend to take a much larger proportion of national incomes than they do in advanced countries. Whatever type of projection is used this item should be brought into the open.

The same is true in principle of defence expenditure, but it clearly applies here only in a very general way, since defence is pre-eminently a political matter. However, an inordinately large defence outlay in a development country is much more likely to be a symptom of the insecurity of the government than a rational provision against external threats. The difficulty is that a level of defence expenditure, once accepted, becomes a particularly strong vested interest, and extremely difficult[1] to reduce. It is only in the most recent period that quantitative methods of evaluating defence expenditure in an objective manner have been introduced in some of the advanced countries.[2]

2. *The Levels of Choice*

The process of drawing up an expenditure programme is an exercise in the allocation of economic resources; that is to say, it is concerned with a series of (marginal) choices between different uses or combinations of land, labour, and capital. We can distinguish four levels (of descending generality) at which this kind of choice has to be made: (i) the first is concerned with the size of the public sector: the choice between leaving resources in the private sector, 'to fructify in the pockets of the taxpayers', and transferring command over them to the public sector; (ii) within the public sector a functional choice has to be made in the

---

1. As is only too evident among the South American countries.
2. Following the pioneer work done at the RAND Corporation, cf. C. J. Hitch and R. McKean, *Economics of Defense in the Nuclear Age*, Harvard University Press, 1960.

allocation of resources between one Ministry or Department and another; (iii) within the purview of each Ministry or Department there is a complex of related expenditures—for instance the different levels (or cycles) of education. Choice has to be made concerning the weights to be given to the different branches; (iv) finally, within a service project—say, additional electricity generation—choice has to be exercised between different techniques—thermal, hydro, or possible nuclear, and also between the sizes of the possible installations (which will depend partly on the technique chosen).

At the highest level of choice the basic problem is the control of resources by the public and private sectors respectively. The most fundamental way of measuring this is by looking at the ratio of public expenditure to the G.N.P. Public expenditure is financed from three sources: profits of commercial undertakings, taxes, and loans. Since trading profits are unlikely to be very large the important decision for the government is the wisdom or otherwise of raising more taxes to finance further public expenditure. This decision will no doubt be made mainly on political grounds, but it clearly has vitally important economic repercussions. If people and firms are prepared to lend voluntarily[1] to the government it will be able to spend more without raising additional taxes. In the next chapter we shall discuss the possibility of achieving this desirable result.

What is at stake is not so much the immediate reaction of taxpayers, but the effect of the expansion of public activity on their future wealth and consequently their ability to pay taxes. This is the *social opportunity cost* of the benefits foregone by choosing one or other allocation of the resources concerned. Although this is particularly obvious at the top level of choice, it is a factor which has to be weighed up in every act of selection.

When planning the allocation of resources between public and private sectors (or for that matter between different functions, such as defence and education), it may be convenient to start with a 'notional total' of what seems reasonable. At a later stage this can be adjusted and given content, as the details of the plan begin to take shape. Is it possible to say in any way what would be an

---

1. Forced (compulsory) loans are advocated by some economists: but the political experience of attempting to implement these has been anything but happy, cf. the Kaldor plans for British Guiana, Ghana, and Turkey, contained in the Reports to the respective governments.

appropriate national total for the whole public sector of a development country? (We may abstract for this purpose from trading services or enterprises, which are free of tax complications.) In a Western welfare state we should expect to find the public sector occupying between 30 and 40 per cent of the national product, nearer the latter than the former. A public sector of this order in a development country would give ample scope for control of the level of activity; but as we saw in the last chapter it would be substantially larger than most development countries have to-day. Moreover, considering the size of the agricultural sector in these countries, which may occupy 60 per cent or more of the G.N.P. (as compared with 5 per cent in the U.K.), and also the extent to which the government of a development country will be engaged on infrastructure work which brings in no immediate return in the early stages of development, something of the order of 20 per cent would seem more realistic.

However inspired the planners, in the last analysis choice at high levels (as has been said) is likely to be made primarily on political or ideological grounds. This is especially likely to be true not only of defence expenditure, but of certain industrial investments which have become status symbols, such as the development of heavy industries, pharmaceuticals, a merchant navy, luxury hotels, or lavish representation abroad. Such assertions of national pride are natural accompaniments of emergence into independence, but it should never be forgotten that they are economically unproductive. Planners must take them into account; but at the same time it is their business to see that they do not absorb so great a volume of resources as to retard the growth of the G.N.P.

It is at the second (inter-functional) level of choice that the most important decisions for growth of the G.N.P. have to be made. On the one side there is the pull of the basic infrastructure projects, and in respect of social services (especially education) this is likely to be very strong indeed; but to realise their full effects these require a span of some twenty years. On the other side there is an urgent need for superstructure projects which will contribute quickly to the flow of final output on which expanding incomes can be spent. Infrastructure will, as we have seen, be almost wholly the reponsibility of the national government, but it is obvious sense for the government to make as much use as it can of other agencies: local governments, voluntary associations and charities, and unpaid community work. The national government's interest in superstructure in a mixed economy will on the other hand for the most part take the form of encouraging production through fiscal incentives and through specific organisations such as an Industrial Development Corporation rather than taking direct responsibility itself.

The problem of time enters into choice in a number of ways: first the choice between projects whose construction period is short and those where it is long; secondly between those whose benefits can be realised quickly on completion and those where the full effect only matures gradually. Dams are examples of long construction projects whose benefits for the most part accrue quickly after completion (if proper utilisation plans have been made in advance). Schools on the other hand are quickly built but their full benefits will only slowly be realised.

At the inter-Ministry level questions of the impact of one line of development on economic opportunities in other lines (overspill) are of great importance. Some projects are in intention multi-purpose. A dam erected primarily to provide power can probably also be used to extend irrigation and so increase the productivity of agriculture. This can be linked with land settlement and reforestation. Other projects, even if not in intention multipurpose, have important overspill effects. Thus a telephone system put in for government purposes can be of great assistance to the tourist trade. Overspill arising in ways like these is not easy to measure, but an attempt should be made, first, to give appropriate weights to the different benefits, and secondly, so far as possible to quantify them. As suggested earlier, in a development country overspill can usually be expected to be favourable. This result may be missed, however, if a wrong (usually too isolated) location is chosen; complementary investments may never come along. Spreading investment too thin in order to please local interests is a common fault of planning.[1] If a very large volume of secondary investment is required before the primary objective can be realised (for instance building a new town), overspill may be lost for a considerable period. Again a new project may destroy the market for a previously prosperous investment. These choices are not necessarily wrong in the same sense as the choice of a faulty location: their appropriateness depends very much on the

1. Faults of this type are now recognised to have been made in the planning of the Italian South.

time-choice implied. The point to emphasise is that overspill should always be carefully looked into, and, other things being equal, the projects with good overspill should have priority.

Experience suggests that below a certain point of infrastructure development the threshold of economic development can hardly be crossed. Just which functions it will be most urgent to concentrate upon depends, naturally, on the type of economy and on its initial provision when the development process starts. One basic difference between advanced and development countries is the flexibility of the former, shown by the ease with which the labour force adapts to changes in economic conditions and techniques, whereas in the latter there tends to be a basic rigidity. Consequently developments which improve the facilities for the movement of people, capital, and goods, and for the spread of ideas, are among the most urgent.

Among the most important of such developments are: (i) the creation of systems of road networks (feeder roads connecting up villages to through roads), and the development of internal airlines; (ii) raising the standard of literacy as a foundation for a balanced educational system; (iii) improving the standard of living of the poorer members of the community, especially in towns, by better food, low income housing schemes, drainage and sewerage, and above all by the provision of a pure water supply; (iv) conquest of the most devastating epidemic and endemic diseases. These improvements are to a considerable extent interrelated. Better communications automatically improve contacts between town and country, and between producers and merchants. Urban problems are greatly complicated by immigration from the country, and a common cause of this is the desire for better educational facilities. A pure water supply will in itself go far to eliminate a number of diseases. Many of these developments can usefully be shared by national and local governments under the general supervision of the national government.

Infrastructure developments of these types have to be financed out of taxation and are slow in yielding their fruits, so that a poor country in the early stages of development must be careful not to spread its net too widely. (Public utilities such as electricity or public transport, which can be made to cover their costs, are in a different category.) It is not inevitable, however, that a development country should have to devote a great deal of public money to all these things. Some peoples need no stimulus to movement; they are natural adventures. The southern Nigerians (especially the Ibos) are a good example of this. In their case population pressure has added a spur to movement; but in other cases it seems to have the opposite effect. Historically the high state of development reached at an early stage by the Greeks can be ascribed to ease of communication by sea, and to a good system of education. The remarkable growth and adaptability of the Japanese economy in the present century had a similar foundation. Japan, however, reached a high degree of development with a minimum of land communication: a good but slender railway system, and only a rudimentary provision of roads. By following this policy in the early stages of development the Japanese minimised the burden of the communications system on tax revenue; but they did so at the cost of subsequent road chaos. It is worth remembering also that compulsory primary education was not introduced in England until 1870, about a century after the 'Industrial Revolution', when development was already far advanced. But there was in existence a good system of privately provided secondary and higher education.

3. *Choice between Programmes: Agriculture*

It would clearly take us too far afield to discuss even the types of choice that have to be faced in planning these sorts of improvement; but those lying in two particular fields—agriculture and education—are so vital that it will be useful to examine broadly the major areas in which decisions have to be made. To concentrate on agriculture is not to deny that industrialisation may also be important, both for its own sake and as an outlet for surplus labour. But as has been said, so far as public expenditure is concerned, the national government's part in a mixed economy will mainly be to provide incentives. As many of these are financial, they can more conveniently be discussed in the next chapter.

Governments need no stimulus to encourage industrialisation (although their methods are often clumsy and susceptible of improvement). Agricultural promotion, by contrast, has tended to be neglected, at least until recently. This is a great mistake. The traditional techniques of production used in most development countries are primitive and inefficient, so that the returns from improvements will be very high indeed. Moreover, many of them can bring about an increase in the supply of consumers' goods without costly investment and in a relatively short space of time—perhaps within a single crop year. They are consequently a most important way of increasing the supply of final products before the major development projects are ready to do so. Another advantage of agriculture is that it is naturally labour intense. It is true that with the old techniques much of the labour working in the fields tends to be redundant (at least seasonally); in most cases the best line of improvement lies not so much in drawing off labour from agriculture, as in employing it more intensively. It is notable that in Japan where there has been spectacular improvement in agricultural output since the 1940's the labour force has scarcely diminished. Thus even after improvement agriculture will remain a labour intense industry.

The proper objectives of agricultural promotion in development countries are two: success in export markets and a better home food supply. There may be a very difficult problem of choice between them, but on the whole the two developments can be complementary. General improvements in the interests of food supply will also improve export crops. It is important for countries with export crop facilities to take measures to improve the quality of those already produced (for competition gets fiercer year by year), and to experiment in order to extend the range. There are undoubtedly a number of world traded products—tropical tree crops and meat and dairy products—which can be successfully grown in a number of places where they have not traditionally been grown for export. Examples would be East African tea and Sudan cotton. But generally speaking, to break into world markets with such crops is a fairly difficult process which takes time. With the enlarged possibilities of rapid transport, however, a much extended range of products can enter into world trade, so that the opportunities are wide for the export of food crops which are also grown in the interests of the home market.

In most development countries a better supply of food for the home market should have a very high priority. There is overwhelming evidence that the first thing people want to buy as they get a little better off is more and better food. This is not surprising in view of the fact that the dietary of the mass of the people in most development countries is either absolutely insufficient or at least unbalanced, with a shortage of protein. With the process of urbanisation and industrialisation an additional need for food arises, since urban occupations require more stamina than primitive farming, and factory workers have no opportunity of growing their own food.

The precise crops or forms of animal husbandry that a government should encourage depend on local conditions; but there are numerous factors common to all agricultural improvement in development countries. Several of these belong essentially to the infrastructure and must be the concern of the national government.

In the first place steps should be taken to find which are the most appropriate crops—as a result of soil analysis (which will probably call for the help of foreign experts) and climatic recording. Secondly, basic works common to a whole area need to be undertaken: first of all, improved water supply for irrigation, either by canal or overhead system. With 'dry' farming it is probable that only one crop a year can be grown; with irrigation this may well be raised to three. As a result of soil analysis other works such as drainage, bunding, and anti-erosion measures may also prove to be desirable. The third necessity is the introduction (and generalisation) of better 'raw materials': seeds or clones, better breeds of farm animals, and so on. Before the most appropriate types can be chosen experimentation and perhaps special breeding will be required. None of these measures are likely to produce their full potential without much patient help (not merely advice) from extension workers.[1] Large numbers of these will need to be available.

The next problem is to secure more bountiful harvests in every crop. Increased agricultural productivity can take the form either of more output per acre or more output per man-hour. In the early stages of development when abundant manpower is still available on farms the former is the more important. In this field of development experience shows that the most striking improvements can be brought about on the one hand by pest destruction and on the other by a proper use of appropriate fertilisers. Means for both of these are now freely available in a way that was unthinkable even ten years ago. Japanese experience suggests that of these two the destruction of pests is slightly the more productive, for the reason that, besides saving crops which would otherwise have been lost, it provides a much greater latitude in the choice

1. Where mixed farming is practised either the extension workers need to be all round experts, or a detailed programme of crop management must be laid down. Experience shows that farmers may become quite confused by the variety of advice showered upon them, some of it often inconsistent because oriented to a particular crop.

of crops and of sowing times. Only a fraction of the gain from better crops will be realised, however, unless adequate care is taken with such processing as may be necessary and with grading and marketing. For this authoritative instruction will probably also be necessary; but it will pay very high dividends, not only in better market results (especially for export), but also as an encouragement to greater production.

There remains one more area where choice has to be made, and it is often a very difficult choice, charged with political implications: that of the steps necessary to secure the fullest possible utilisation of land. These include applying the right stimulus for greater effort or, it may be, penalty for bad utilisation. (As we shall discuss later this is a field where fiscal measures may prove effective.) To secure proper utilisation it may be necessary to undertake extensive land reform.[1] For the landowner who does not adequately use his land a break up of estates may be indicated. For the little man it means help with acquiring a consolidated holding (thus avoiding waste of time and land), and real security of tenure. Only when adequate security is available will it be possible for organisations such as co-operatives and marketing boards to supply the full financial assistance needed.

It is between these various measures that choice has to be made in order to promote agricultural improvement. There are many routes leading to the same objectives, and each country has to choose those which are most appropriate to both its natural potentialities and to the traditions of its farming population.

4. *Choice within an integrated Service: Education*

The discussion of agricultural improvement has already brought us into the area of the third level of choice: between different elements within a given function or Ministry. One of the most important fields for decisions at this level is in the development of an educational system. The importance of making correct decisions in this field can hardly be exaggerated. With the possible exception of defence, education is normally the largest object of public outlay in any country, whether advanced or developing. There are two special problems in the field of education which need to be kept continually in mind. In the first place the results

---

1. This was an important element in the Japanese situation, cf. R. P. Dore, '*Land Reform in Japan*', Oxford, 1959. The Japanese were lucky in being able to pass off the political onus to the occupying Americans.

of a programme of educational development will only fully be realised over a period of twenty years or so. This implies a long sustained increase in the tax burden, so that there is a special need for wise spending. More fundamentally, it implies that whatever period is chosen for the general development plan, the educational programme must have a long period reference. But over a period of this length the whole economic appearance of a country may be changed. National income might conceivably have doubled, and the economic structure would certainly have changed drastically. Consequently, however difficult it may be, efforts must be made to foresee the course of development sufficiently to provide in a general way for the skills and other needs of the future. This implies that educational planning cannot be divorced from general economic planning. If it is organised in a self-contained direction the education system will not contribute as much as it should do to the growth of the G.N.P.[1]

The second peculiarity of education is the close relation that the successive stages, or levels, of education bear to each other. Their relative weights are not arbitrary, but mutually dependent. A primary system so overstretched that an appropriate secondary system cannot be afforded leads to waste and frustration. Universities not supported by an adequate secondary level cannot attain a satisfactory standard. University curricula not tied to the plan of secondary education will produce unwanted skills and the depressing spectacle of the unemployed graduate. Finally, the whole structure will fail in its purpose if it is not supplied with an adequately trained teaching staff at all stages. The educational system is the producer of a skilled labour force; but it is also one of the largest users of the educated manpower of the economy.

A basic difficulty in planning an educational system is that education is both a consumer's and a producer's good. It shares with the development of communications the honour of being the best solvent of traditional rigidities—notwithstanding that some educational systems are still (unfortunately) geared to preserve tradition rather than to stimulate progress. A well conceived educational ladder can also do important work in bridging income differentials. Not all the peoples of development countries are yet alive to what education can do for them. Where this is so some preliminary work may have to be organised to persuade the

---

1. For further discussion see my article 'The Economics of Educational Expansion in Low Income Countries', *Three Banks Review*, March 1965.

general public of its advantages. Generally speaking, however, governments find that the promise of a large development of education is a highly popular move. Indeed education is publicised as a 'fundamental human right'. Approached only from this angle an educational programme may easily become unbalanced. It is evident that on this approach there can be no rational choice.

No one will deny that education can make an important, even vital, contribution to economic growth; but in what way it operates to this end is not obvious and is hardly amenable to quantitative measurement, although attempts have been made.[1] The contribution of education to growth can operate in two quite separate ways. On the one hand the system can be consciously geared to produce particular skills which are certain to be in demand. On the other it is one of the most important elements in creating a flexible labour force that can adapt itself quickly to changes in economic opportunity. In this respect it should not be overlooked that Japan introduced universal primary education in 1872, only two years later than the U.K. The Japanese economy unquestionable owes much of its remarkable flexibility to this long experience.

If we may suggest a rational procedure in educational choice we might start with a 'notional total' reflecting the social opportunity cost (at the margin) between education and other developments such as public health. The total also needs to be considered from the beginning in terms of money costs, because of the burden that education throws on the revenue and the difficulty of expanding taxes (these are questions that we shall be considering at a later stage). After this comes the choice of the relative importance to be given to the different educational stages, remembering that each successive stage is very much more expensive than the last. This choice needs to be related to the present position of education in the country, for instance in respect of voluntary provision. It also needs to be related to the per capita national income. The advanced countries find that they have to spend 4 to 5 per cent of their G.N.P. on education in order to keep up. For a country

---

1. For instance by the so-called 'residual method': the income differential between advanced and development countries, and the faster growth of the former, cannot be fully explained by differences in inputs of economic resources. There remains a residue, which it is asserted is mainly due to the influence of education. Clearly this is important, but there are a number of other factors to consider, such as the effect of technical innovations, large scale production and so on.

whose total public sector does not amount to more than about 12 per cent of the G.N.P. this would be a tall order, but it is a target nevertheless that it should put before itself.

In choosing the appropriate relation between educational levels some use can be made of the experience of countries that have proceeded farther along the road to development. It is the view of U.N.E.S.C.O. (after the study of a number of countries) that the ratio of the total numbers receiving primary, secondary, and higher education respectively should be of the order of 100:22:2.[1] In choosing the primary programme, consequently, allowance must also be made for the higher stages. Nor should the programme be so tight that it leaves no room for adult education, literacy campaigns, and special opportunities for women and girls to catch up with the general educational level. The relation between the stages determines the number of teachers required at each level, it being the aim to employ only trained teachers in primary schools and only graduates at the secondary level. The universities will of course require highly trained specialists.

Capital costs of the building and equipment of schools also have to be considered. At the primary level these can be very modest. Substantial school buildings are not required in the tropics, and they can probably be erected by voluntary effort. It is common experience that 90 per cent or more of the cost of primary schools consists of teachers' salaries. Secondary schools, however, are costly. Their equipment is also expensive, and a substantial part of it may have to be imported, especially for science laboratories. (This is a level of choice which calls for special care. The fact that the advanced countries use very elaborate equipment in their school laboratories does not prove that, given a good teacher, a great deal of progress cannot be made with quite simple equipment.) The time is probably past when university buildings needed to be grandiose in order to persuade people of their importance; but they are inevitably still more costly than secondary school buildings, especially as it will probably be desired to make them largely residential. At these upper stages educational building will be competing hotly with other capital works (such as roads and housing) for the scarce supplies of labour and materials in the construction industries. Social opportunity cost then becomes very relevant.

1. Some years ago Sir Arthur Lewis suggested (in relation to Ghana) the ratio 100:8 for the first two levels. This, however, was before the special demands of development had become apparent.

Having got thus far in programme building, it is necessary to look more closely at the content of the different stages. In choosing the primary programme the rate of population growth is vital. Where population is increasing rapidly the proportion of school age children in the population will be abnormally high. It has been estimated that in terms of the G.N.P. the cost of educating a given percentage of the relevant age group may be ten times as high as in an advanced country. Some economies can be made, for instance by cutting down the length of the course (but lasting literacy can hardly be guaranteed with less than a six years' course), or by working double shifts (but this is socially undesirable). To cut down on the calibre of the teachers is self-defeating. Bored children tend to stay away from school and to drop out before the end of the course. In view of these difficulties it must be faced that universal primary education may not be possible without destroying the balance of the stages until after the lapse of some years. A programme of gradual expansion to the target should, however, be possible from the first.

It is at the secondary stage that the choices most vital for the growth of the G.N.P. have to be made. An attempt must be made to forecast the main features of the economy of the future: its rate of growth on the average and in particular directions. (This part of the exercise belongs mainly to the central planning authority, but the need for close co-ordination of the education programme with the rest of the Plan is obvious.) The rate of growth envisaged by the Plan provides a basic guide line for educational development. But since initially this will be insufficient for needs, education expansion should proceed more rapidly than the growth rate at first; eventually it will flatten out. It is generally found that a double stream of secondary education will be desirable: a long course for those who go on to higher education and a shorter course to cater for the very large demand for middle grade technicians, engineers, clerical and scientific workers. In addition short technical courses will probably be required.

At the higher stages equally important decisions have to be made; but the numbers involved will be much smaller. The first question is at what stage the transfer from school to university should take place. In view of its cost, it is much more economical to reserve university training for those who can really profit from it than to accept large numbers and subsequently send away those who cannot make the grade. This policy, however, calls for a really high standard in the top forms at school if the universities are to receive a satisfactory entry. A second fundamental decision (owing to the specialised nature of university courses) concerns the right numbers to be admitted to the different Faculties, and in particular the choice between the humanities and the sciences. In the past in very many countries the latter have been neglected, partly no doubt because of the cost of equipment, so that the unemployed graduate has always been an arts man. At the same time there are many skills whose training formally comes into the arts category which are certain to be in demand, not least those of economists and statisticians. For a development country that will only have a small entry for the higher skills it is a legitimate economy to send the top people for training abroad, preferably at the post graduate level. This applies in particular to medical training. Teaching hospitals need to be very large to cover all the skills required, and they are inordinately expensive.

It is more than likely that these exercises (difficult enough in any case) will be rendered more so by the inadequacy of the relevant statistics, both of the size and growth of the population and of the relative demands for different skills. Some guidance can be gleaned concerning the latter from the experience of similar economies which have reached a higher stage of development; even if the result is rough it will still be better than if no attempt had been made to quantify the forecasts. A well chosen structure should permit sufficient flexibility to adjust to needs as they arise. There is a further problem, however. Educational demands may be correctly foreseen; but is there any guarantee that parents and children will conform to them? The pull towards education for white collar jobs is endemic in all countries, and the means of making known the probable developments of demand are far less good in development than in advanced countries. Publicity and guidance by teachers will doubtless help. In addition it is well to establish scholarship ladders in the directions required. Short of compulsion, the more freely the market mechanism is allowed to operate on wages and salaries, the easier will it be to get children into the right places.

5. *Choice within a non-integrated Service: Public Health*

The examples of agriculture and educational development illustrate the kinds of decisions that have to be made at the three top levels of choice. If space allowed, the same process could be carried through for other services. Something, however, should be said concerning choice in the field of public health, since this is almost as vital for development as education. Indeed some countries actually give it priority over education. Apart from the basic decision as to how much health and medical service should be provided in relation to other public outlay, the choices to be made are not quite so exacting as in the education field, because the different parts of health and medical services are less mutually dependent on each other than are the stages of education. More of any of them will be useful, irrespective of the provision of the others.

There are, however, two sorts of choice particularly relevant to the health services. The first concerns the relative weight to be given to the different branches of the services; the second has to do with the location of different treatment centres. Health services fall into three broad categories: preventive (including environmental) services, curative services, and research. Clearly in a development country the scope for this last named is likely to be severely limited by the shortage of skilled personnel: but, as we have seen (Ch.1, p. 2), research into local diseases may transcend in importance the interests of the country where it is carried out. It should consequently not be difficult to obtain funds and research workers from abroad.

As regards the other two branches of the service, most countries experience a persistent demand for curative, and an indifference to preventive, services. This is not the right way round. It is cheaper, and more pleasant for the potential patient, to save him from catching a disease than to treat him when he has fallen a victim to it. Moreover, in most development countries the supply of adequately trained nurses who can be trusted to look after patients properly (and not charge privately for the simplest conveniences) is even more backward than that of teachers. This is not to imply that the supply of doctors is fully adequate, but fewer are needed and generally speaking there has been more effort to provide them.

The crux of the location choice is whether it is better to set up a large number of small treatment centres (clinics, maternities, leprosaria, and so on), so that most people will be within fairly easy reach of what they need, or to concentrate on a smaller number of larger units where more skilled attention can be given. In the education service the small school is always at a disadvantage (though with modern transport there is no compelling reason why this should persist). Exactly the opposite may well be true of health services. Early treatment (for minor accidents, for instance) is essential in the tropics, so that a wide scatter of small centres is of real advantage. Given a little encouragement most villages can provide themselves with an ambulance for more serious cases.[1]

6. *The Application of Cost/Benefit Analysis*

In our discussion of decision making at the three upper levels of choice it has been implicit that rational choice consists every time in selecting the alternative that offers the greatest net benefit. This calls for some elucidation. The principle can be seen most clearly in decisions relating to the fourth level of choice, between alternative techniques for attaining a given result: such as employing more or less labour intense techniques, using different motive power to make electricity, applying different types of irrigation, and so on. It is at this stage that the best hope of quantification exists, although the principles involved are no different at the higher levels of choice.

The first step in quantifying choice is to list the project costs that will have to be incurred for construction and operation of each alternative. The point of time when it is expected that the costs will be incurred should be carefully noted, since this is essential for the calculation. The costs listed should stretch as far into the future as is relevant—which may be for the lifetime of the equipment, but (as we shall discuss below) is also related to the possibilities of

---

1. *Note:* The public expenditure so far discussed (save for possible education grants to scholars) has all been in the field of buying goods and services from the private sector. In an advanced welfare state such as the U.K. only some 50 per cent of the expenditure on social services consists of purchases of goods and services, the rest consists of social transfers out of taxation. These may take the form of outlay transfers (which enable consumers' goods—such as milk or eggs —to be bought below cost). The larger part, however, are income transfers— money grants to persons. No development country is likely to be able to afford a large volume of social transfers. Indeed they should be very careful about committing themselves, since almost all of these commitments are 'open-ended' in the sense that a guarantee of payments is implied whenever certain stated conditions are fulfilled. Some development countries, however, have got themselves enmeshed in outlay transfers in an effort to prevent the prices of certain basic foodstuffs from rising. Such a policy is self-defeating. If output of the food in question rises, the budgetary burden tends to become intolerable, so that no effort will be devoted to increasing productivity, and home supplies may well have to be supplemented by imports.

obsolescence, if these can be foreseen with any confidence. This cost stream then has to be confronted with a similar stream of expected benefits, likewise dated according to the period in which it is estimated that they will accrue. Only in respect of projects of a commercial nature is it possible to put a direct money value on the benefit side. For other types of project recourse must be had to evaluation of efficiency in real terms: so many school places, patient bed-nights, and so on. To complete the exercise some more or less conventional pricing system must be used. In order to put them on a comparable footing these two streams must then be discounted down to the present. The alternative which shows the greater present value excess of benefits over costs will be the right one to choose. Only by discounting to the present can allowance be made for the fact that benefits which will be enjoyed only some time ahead are not so attractive as those which can be quickly enjoyed, while costs which will only have to be incurred some years hence will be easier to bear than those which have to be shouldered right away (more especially as there should be larger supplies of all sorts which can then be drawn upon).

The crucial decision concerns the rate of discount which is to be used for this exercise. The higher the rate chosen the more quick-maturing investments will appear attractive in relation to long gestation projects, and vice versa. Hence the rate to be chosen depends on when it is most desired that the benefits should accrue. This is usually referred to as *social time preference*. In a development country when supplies of all sorts of equipment are meagre and the expectation of life is still short, it would be natural to suppose that a high social time preference rate of discount would be appropriate. In a well equipped advanced country it might be expected to be substantially lower. It may be that in a development country the government feels a greater concern for future generations than does the present population; but to fly in the face of a rational time preference by loading the Plan with long gestation projects, to the detriment of quick maturing benefits, would be, at the very least, arbitrary. Yet this in fact is often done, though for the most part perhaps more from the use of faulty methods of calculation than from any desire to influence unduly social time preference.

Since the comparison of present values is to be used as a yardstick to choose between alternatives, the same rate of discount must clearly be used for all choices at a particular time. Over the years, however, the appropriate rate of discount may alter quite substantially. One would expect it to fall as provision becomes more abundant and the expectation of life extends, save in so far as these changes may be counteracted by a very rapid growth of population, calling for a quick expansion of housing, food, education, and other services for children. It should be noted that the net benefit must be defined as the cash flow of benefits *net* of actual outgoings, without distinction between current and capital account, as would be done in budget accounting. In the early years, when the main construction costs have to be met, the net benefit will no doubt be heavily negative, but the position will later be reversed.

It will be observed that in this discussion of the rate of discount, depending on social time preference, no mention has been made of the rate of interest at which funds can be borrowed. In fact neither the market rate of interest nor any lower rate which may be offered by a lender has any fundamental role to play in problems of rational choice. The rate of interest in this sense appears merely as one item in the cost stream, and probably rather a minor one. The fact that a loan for a particular project is offered at a low rate does not of itself make the project more worthwhile. That depends always on total benefits less total costs.

It emerges from the above discussion that it is convenient in planning the expenditure structure to approach it from two ends. At the macro end we have our notional totals: first of public versus private expenditure, the public sector then being broken down into totals for Ministries and departments, and thence to the optimum relation between the different elements of a complex service. Starting from the micro end, planning within a Ministry or department, the 'admissible' projects (in the sense of those which would show an excess of benefit over cost in the absence of a budgetary constraint) can then be listed on a broad estimate of relative net benefits. As many as possible of these are then to be fitted within the Ministry notional total, taking account of the appropriate relation with other elements in the service in question, and of the Ministry's other commitments.

Outlay on new construction inevitably varies very much from year to year, according to the time profile of inputs of labour and materials; but periods of special strain or relative ease should be foreseeable, if good adherence is kept to the planned time schedules. The non-development element of public expenditure should follow a far steadier trend. For the most part it should be possible to allow this to progress smoothly, and budgetary provision should be made accordingly. If particular strains arise it may be permissible slightly to postpone certain outlays, such as repairs and replacements, in the interests of preserving balance in the economy. Imbalance arising out of expenditure is, however, closely related to the type of financing that is used, and to this problem we must now turn.

CHAPTER THREE

FINANCE & THE FINANCIAL
INFRASTRUCTURE

1. *The Need for a Financial Programme*

CHOOSING the appropriate methods of finance cannot make a bad plan good, but it can make it better. Using the wrong methods can wreck even the best of plans. The incomings side of the account calls for just as much attention as the outgoings side. Moreover, it has a special contribution of its own to make to the process of development, by smoothing out fluctuations on the one hand and by providing incentives for investment on the other. Far too often finance has been the cinderella of planners, in the sense that what passes as an adequate array of taxing and borrowing suggestions has been trumped up at the end to look respectable, instead of being thought out alongside, to match the expenditure structure.

In a development country financial policy has to concern itself with three different elements. In the first place there must be adequate provision for existing services, including the maintenance of non-revenue producing capital assets. Provision for this should be large enough to ensure that there is no deterioration in the quality of a service as it expands either deliberately or through natural increase. Natural increase alone can be formidable in such services as education and housing, especially where the rate of population growth is high. Further, state employees must be granted increments (creep) as they get older. It may well be necessary also to offer higher remuneration to secure the additional personnel who will be wanted for expanded services, in view of the scarcity of trained labour. If trade unionism is well developed there are additional complications. If in addition the prices of home produced consumers' goods are allowed to rise substantially (especially food and cotton cloth) the situation may become chaotic. It is the duty of financial policy to prevent this sort of sequence; but it is only one of the jobs it has to undertake.

In the second place finance has to be planned so as to cover development expenditure in the widest sense, including fixed capital formation and the necessary co-operating working capital and labour. There must also be adequate provision for stocks, spares, and minor replacements (which will come on current account). Development of all kinds calls for expanded training and research facilities.

The third element of financial policy consists in laying an appropriate financial infrastructure, which is just as important as an adequate physical one. There are some development countries, such as India, where the financial foundation was laid many years ago. But it may well not be geared to the special requirements of development and therefore need substantial overhauling. In newly independent countries brought up on the Currency Board system, the financial infrastructure has to be built up from the bottom, as an essential ingredient in the process of growth. We shall examine below the steps that need to be taken to this end.

Broadly there are three methods of finance open to most development countries: (a) gifts and grants; (b) loans; (c) taxes and other current receipts such as the profits of public enterprise. To ensure stability taxes and other current home revenue should cover all the needs we have specified above under the first heading, and in addition contribute something towards development.[1] The remainder will have to be met by borrowing of one form or another, together with any gifts or grants that may be forthcoming.

The basic economic distinction between sources of finance is between domestic and foreign provision. The vital element is home finance, and it is this which calls particularly for a special policy, although, with the many sources of external finance now available to development countries, there is need of careful policy in that field also. External finance is usually considered indispensable, and there is no doubt that it can lead to more rapid development if it is wisely used. But in whatever form it comes it tends to bring with it certain embarrassments and disadvantages.

Fortunate is the country that can manage its development without external borrowing. England in the period of her most rapid growth succeeded in doing so; Japan has managed with only a minimum of overseas aid. More recently Russia has financed her very rapid growth entirely from domestic resources. 'Operation boot strap' in Puerto Rico is another recent example. But none of these countries was undeveloped in the modern sense at the time when its rapid growth began. And it is important to remember

1. For further discussion see below, p. 171.

that the cost in human suffering of the acceleration of their rate of growth was often very great indeed.

2. *Finance from Abroad: Aid and Loan*

Finance from abroad now usually comes in the form of 'aid'— funds (or the equivalent) transferred to development countries with the express purpose of helping them to develop, and without the expectation of a full market return. In the nineteenth century things were very different. Foreign aid was of two sorts: first, loans arranged by bankers and finance houses and subscribed in Europe, often carrying fantastically high rates of interest.[1] More reasonably, in the second place, funds could be raised on the London Stock Exchange, either directly or through the intermediary of finance houses. For Commonwealth borrowers slightly easier terms were available under the Colonial Stock Acts; but by and large a market rate of return was expected. In the 1920's a large amount of lending was carried through, by the United States mainly, in Latin American countries; but this was also at market rates, which were then very high. When the slump came most of these countries were in default.

Gifts in kind and money grants are two types of aid which are often more or less interchangeable. Quantitatively they are not very important, but they do have the advantage that they leave no aftermath of debt service, as do loans. Gifts of real assets take such forms as ships, fishing vessels, industrial equipment, on occasions even a complete steel mill. Many grants are 'tied' in the sense that it is a condition that the funds are spent on particular equipment in the grant-giving country. Again, grants merge into 'soft loans', funds lent at a low rate of interest, perhaps no more than 1 per cent, and with a waiver of repayment and interest for a period of years. If these are also tied to particular purchases the low rate of interest may be completely misleading, depending on the charge made for the equipment in the lending country. In general it is reckoned that a tied grant or loan which is arranged on a unilateral basis may reduce the value of the aid by as much as 20 per cent.

The policy of the aid-giving countries has fluctuated over the years since 1945. In the early postwar period there was a tendency

---

1. cf. D. S. Landes, *Bankers and Pashas*, Heinemann, 1958 (the financing of Egyptian investment under the Khalif Ismail). That rates of 20 per cent or so were demanded was partly due to utter ignorance of the situation.

to prefer grants, perhaps because the memory of the widespread default on loan service in the early 1930's was still fresh. With the growth of aid from international agencies, loans have become predominant since a reasonable rate of return must be assured in order to maintain the inflow of funds to the agency. In any case loans are sometimes preferred by development countries because they are suspicious of the motives which prompt gifts and grants.

We can distinguish at least three dominant motives behind the offer of this sort of aid bilaterally. In the first place there is a sense of obligation and continuing responsibility on the part of former mother countries for ex-colonies that have had to be given their independence, even when it is clear that (on account of small size or poor resources) they are not viable even on current account without a very drastic fall in the standard of living to which they have become accustomed. Aid then takes the form of a grant towards balancing the budget (at a later stage we shall consider the best way in which such aid can be awarded). A striking example of this form of grant is the aid given by France to her former colonies in equatorial Africa; this mainly takes the form of funds to pay for the services of French administrators, the countries themselves not yet being able to supply the requisite trained personnel. More recently the U.K. agreed to underwrite the economy of Nyasaland as it emerged into independent Malawi.

Similar motives may dominate the giving of grants specifically for development rather than for current services. These may range from mixed capital formation to university fees (such as the British Commonwealth Development and Welfare grants, or the French grants from the Caisse d'Outremer). Gifts and grants of this nature are mainly government to government affairs: but the extensive aid given by the great American institutions such as the Ford and Rockefeller Foundations falls essentially into this class, as also does the aid given by various countries under the Colombo Plan. In all of this there is a very big element of altruism, notwithstanding that other motives may also be present.

Grants of this nature merge imperceptibly into aid whose main purpose is political. An international political motive is, however, not infrequently bound up with an internal economic motive. Gifts are frequently due to the wish to help some particular pocket of unemployment at home. If the beneficiary accepts the gift (and he will be under strong pressure to do so) he must also accept the type of equipment offered and the timing of the gift, even if the one is expensive to maintain and the other inconvenient in relation to other plans. Again, some advanced countries (especially the U.S.A.) have handed over surplus foodstuffs, to the great benefit of some poor countries; but the origin of the surpluses was to improve the profits of home farmers, not to feed the starving in development countries.

In all aid of this type the presence of a genuine altruistic element should not be belittled. Nevertheless development countries would do well to ponder the motives which lie behind the proffered gift, even to the point of politely refusing it if it is inappropriate to their needs. Such gifts are often mutually exclusive. If the offer of, say, a deep water harbour from one country is accepted it will probably not be possible to accept another, perhaps cheaper or more convenient, from somewhere else. It should be remembered also that gifts of this nature tend very much to be confined to the actual equipment; but this (as we have seen) is usually only a nucleus. Complementary expenditure, on land, site, and co-operating labour, will, together with maintenance, impose a continuing drain on the development country's finances. Care should consequently always be taken to see that a gift is consistent with the Plan and will not withdraw resources from more important uses.

Much the same arguments apply to bilateral soft loans. Their offer is likely to be due to a mixture of political 'benevolence' and promotion of exports, by making it a condition of the loan that equipment and materials should be purchased in the lending country. This type of loan has greatly increased in popularity among the advanced countries with the decline in overseas sellers' markets and the consequent increase in competitive striving for exports. There is the further consideration that once a certain type of equipment has been installed spares and replacements must normally be ordered from the same source. In respect of consumers' goods also habits may become so fixed that other forms of equipment are unacceptable.[1]

By far the most important type of loan aid to development countries now comes from the World Bank and its agencies, especially the International Development Agency (I.D.A.). There is every prospect that this trend will continue. To start with, the Bank's loans were all of the project type similar to the bilateral aid we have been

---

1. Thus British type metal windows which find a ready sale in Nigeria or Ghana cannot be sold in the former French colonies, which have become accustomed to French types.

discussing. More recently, as a result of greater ease in its finances, the Bank has been prepared to give loans for a mixture of projects, including infrastructure development, so that some of the loans have become virtually non-specific.

Loans from international agencies have several advantages for development countries over those from individual sources. In the first place feasibility studies and expert advice in the physical planning are included. Secondly (and increasingly), allowance is made for supplementary costs and co-operating labour, although in the nature of the case (for instance when a new factory town has to be built before full advantage can be taken of a new hydro-electric works) it is not always possible to do this completely. (Hence the receiving country still needs to do its overspill accounts carefully.) Thirdly, the Bank's loans are not tied in the sense that the equipment must be purchased in a particular country, although the type of equipment to be used may be specified. Against these advantages I.D.A. loans are sometimes very slow in coming to hand, essentially because fresh investigations are required to be made at each phase of a project. Hence their time profile is not easy to fit in with other developments. A good bilateral loan may well be completed more quickly.[1] Quick completion is of first importance so that a project can begin to earn profits and cover its own loan service at the earliest possible moment.

A recent and most promising idea is the use of 'consortia' or groups of financial interests from a number of advanced countries (perhaps four or more), which are prepared to back certain projects jointly, normally those whose total costs are so large that they could not easily be handled by a single concern. Consortia may be got together on the initiative of the Bank, in which case their co-operation is virtually an extension of the work which the Bank is already doing. But a consortium may also be formed on the initiative of individual countries. An interesting result of this form of lending is that it can combine the advantages of bilateral and multilateral aid. The different parts of the project are divided up, and members of the consortium can bid for one or more contracts. The receiving country takes its choice between them, buys in the best market, and is not tied to the products of a particular country. The chance of getting contracts gives a strong incentive for the advanced countries to join the consortium.

1. But dark tales are told of a Russian steel mill for Iraq which never got out of its packing cases.

As we have seen, the London Stock Exchange was an important source of development finance at the turn of the century. Many of the loans were floated directly by the developing countries. Others were arranged by 'Investment Trusts' organised by particular interests in the lending country. A large number were geared to the expansion overseas of primary products in demand in the industrial countries. It was a considerable advantage of direct borrowing on the stock exchange that the funds could be applied to any purpose without restriction. Japan was a very successful borrower in London in this way. The government raised the money on the security of tax revenues, and then transferred the funds to firms and industries, at a time when local savings were insufficient to finance rapid growth. The Australian states were also large borrowers on London; but the allocation of funds was not always wise and led to many defaults, until borrowing was centralised under the (Commonwealth) Loans Board.

Stock exchange loans (now both in London and New York) are still a possible source of development finance. Some use continues to be made of them, especially by smaller countries such as the West Indian Islands. Stock exchanges have, however, lost much of their former attractiveness, partly because of the wide range of facilities now available, partly because the stock exchanges themselves have become much less flexible. They are now expected to operate primarily in the interests of internal credit control. In London both the rate of interest to be offered and the issue price of a loan are dictated by the Capital Issues Committee (an outlier of the Bank of England). Overseas borrowers must take their turn in the queue with British local authorities and other similar bodies. If the wait is a long one an awkward problem of accumulating bank advances and short borrowing for the finance of capital works may arise.[1]

Thus many and various opportunities for finance from abroad are now available to development countries. But it must be remembered that all loans carry with them the problem of debt service. In the early years of the present century, and again in the interwar period, this became a very serious problem. The lessons of that experience seem largely to have been forgotten until very recently, when the problem has once again forced itself upon international consciousness. No doubt the shortness of memory is largely due

1. See my report as Fiscal Commissioner on the Federation of the East Caribbean Territories, cit.

to the fact that in the early postwar years the development countries found themselves in a very favourable position as regards debt
service. Countries like India, which had borrowed heavily in the
nineteenth and early twentieth century, were able to pay off almost
all their debt out of high incomes made during the war. (In
addition India emerged from the war with sterling balances running into thousands of million sterling.) In the prewar period the
West African territories had not yet much demand for loans (the
progress of tropical medicine not having yet made them practicable for development). In the early postwar years they were able
to accumulate very large reserves in times of European food shortages, by the transactions of their commodity Marketing Boards.
(In a sense these territories were temporary net lenders on London,
where the reserves were invested.) Within a decade, however, the
situation had swung back to its accustomed position, and many
development countries now find themselves in a precarious situation. A short run palliative can be found by fresh borrowing in
order to pay the interest on earlier loans; but such a policy cannot
continue indefinitely.

There are only two effective ways in which a country that has
overborrowed can extricate itself from its difficulties. Either
export income must increase sufficiently to carry the burden of the
debt, in addition to providing for essential imports, or domestic
output must rise sufficiently to enable additional tax revenue to be
raised, out of which the government can provide the requisite
funds. Neither of these solutions is likely to be easy. At the same
time for most development countries neither should be quite impossible,[1] if they make a determined effort, and do not relax in the
comforting belief that the advanced countries can be relied on to
supply ever increasing aid, on political if not on humanitarian
or economic grounds.

3. *Finance from Abroad: Direct Investment*

Borrowing from abroad implies the transfer of the savings
generated in the advanced countries to the needs of development
countries. There is also a further channel through which such a
transfer can be accomplished: by direct investment (as distinct
from portfolio buying of securities) by foreign firms setting up

1. cf. J. R. Hicks, *The Social Framework*, Oxford, 3rd ed., 1960, Ch. XII,
for an analysis of the growth of an export surplus as an aftermath of borrowing.

factories or services in development countries. This practice is by no means new. In the nineteenth century, in South America and many other countries, railways, telegraphs, and other public utilities were established by foreign firms, to the great advantage of the countries concerned, which could not have afforded the investments themselves. But the companies remained essentially foreign enclaves, without local roots. In view of the wind of political change it is perhaps not surprising that most of these installations have either been nationalised or transferred to local control, with or without compensation for the capital invested, and often with the result of a serious fall in the quality of the services provided.[1]

Under present conditions, when firms apply to make direct investments in developing countries the situation is substantially different even from what it was a generation ago. In the old days firms were interested in little but public utilities, mines, and plantations. Now their interests have greatly widened. The greater number are intent on light industry, making consumers' goods such as tobacco, beer, condensed milk, footwear—to name only a few—or else materials for processing consumers' goods, such as metal containers. Another category consists of firms who apply to explore and exploit mineral resources, such as oil and bauxite. These normally represent a large amount of capital, but obviously they will only apply where there is a reasonable prospect of exploitable minerals. Similar to these are companies who wish to exploit timber resources, mainly for the production of plywood. Finally, a few firms are still interested in plantation products in a broad sense: tea, palm oil, or fruit growing.[2] Of similar types are the investments of the Commonwealth Development Corporation, which, after a number of false starts, now seems to be concentrating with considerable success on public utilities, such as water and telephones.

A substantial number of these new entrants are firms which have become accustomed to operating in development countries. Their factories can be observed (mainly on trading estates or in new towns) in any country in which there is reasonable assurance of stable government and small danger of sudden confiscation or the imposition of arbitrary taxation. An important difference from

1. The experience of the Argentine Railways is a case in point.
2. I am not concerned with the many plantation and mineral firms which are already established in development countries, since for the most part their import of new capital is small. Many, in fact, are disinvesting as fast as they can, in countries that look politically unstable.

earlier conditions is that all these firms come in subject to strict governmental control. They will be assessed to the normal taxes of the country, save for concessions which are very commonly offered to new firms (we need not discuss these here as we shall be dealing with them in Chapter 5). The government of the development country can (and should) take powers to inspect all books. If they make a success, direct investment of this sort by foreign firms can be of very great advantage to development countries. They bring in the know-how with the capital. Moreover, they provide the quickest route for enlarging the supply of consumers' goods on which the new high incomes generated by the development process can be spent. And there is no burden of debt service implied. (We shall discuss later some problems in connection with remittances to the country of origin.)

Not all companies that start up in a development country, however, make a success of the venture. This may be due to an undervaluation of the very considerable risks involved, both on the supply and demand sides. (I am abstracting from the possibility that the development country may go back on its undertakings, perhaps because of a change of government.) But ill success may be due to the fact that the company is itself a poor risk. It applies mainly because it is captivated by the incentives offered; but it would be unlikely to make much of a success anywhere, and certainly will not be able to break into export markets. Consequently even those development countries most anxious to encourage the entry of foreign firms in order to diversify their economies would do well to observe certain precautions.

In the first place it should always be a condition of granting a permit that a separate local company should be registered—or at least that it should be an entity that keeps separate accounts. If this is done there is a better prospect that there will be a self-contained balance sheet on which taxation can unequivocally be assessed. If the application is by a company wishing to produce and export primary products it should be insisted that as large an amount of processing as possible should be completed within the country: that alumina rather than bauxite should be exported, or that an oil firm should set up a refinery when, say, 5 million tons of crude are being extracted per annum.[1] The main object of this

1. It may also be desirable to seek a guarantee of operation, as in certain circumstances oil companies prefer to leave the oil they have discovered underground as a reserve for considerable periods.

precaution is to secure for the country as much value added as possible; this is both of economic and of fiscal importance. If the company is not well known, with an established reputation, a development country should make very careful enquiries about its previous record. (If this had been done in the past much loss and disappointment might have been avoided.) It must be borne in mind that, unless the home market is potentially large enough to absorb the output of a plant sufficiently large to secure basic economies of scale, export markets will have to be invaded. This implies really high standards of workmanship and marketing. The development country should satisfy itself on all these points before granting a permit.

It is a reinsurance for both parties to the transaction if a partnership can be arranged, in the sense of a joint Board of Directors. The local resident directors would no doubt be suggested by the Industrial Development Corporation (or similar body). If this is done there is no danger of the firm remaining a foreign enclave; it will be part of the structure of the economy. This danger is in any case much smaller than it was. With rapid air communications, once the factory is firmly established, the foreign directors will tend not to reside. They will merely visit the installations from time to time to assure themselves that everything is running smoothly.

This form of borrowing for development is already of considerable importance, and the prospects for its expansion are brightening. It is generally agreed that the easiest way in which the advanced countries can assist the development countries to expand their exports is by accepting a larger volume of simple manufactured goods and processed raw materials.[1]

4. *Home Savings and Deficit Finance*

Useful as is foreign borrowing for the development of most countries, what can be achieved out of home savings is still more important, even if it is quantitatively smaller. It is often asserted that development countries are so poor that domestic savings must in any case be negligible; but this is far from the truth. Even poor Indian peasants have been found to save a substantial proportion of their meagre incomings, voluntarily reducing their living

---

1. cf. Essay by I. G. Patel in 'New Directions of World Trade', a Chatham House Report prepared for the U.N. Conference on Trade and Development, and the Final Act of the Conference, June 1964.

standards almost below subsistence level in order to keep a reserve.[1] West African cocoa farmers were also found[2] to have a high propensity to save. The problem of increasing the flow of home savings for development is consequently a double one: of taking steps actually to increase the volume and of mobilising it into channels where it will be available to the government and other developers. There are almost as many ways of extracting savings from the home population as there are of borrowing the savings of foreigners, quite apart from those which are taken by the government in taxation (with which we are not concerned in the present chapter).

The simplest method of extracting savings for development from the home population is by means of 'deficit finance'[3] whereby the government spends more than it has and covers the shortfall by borrowing, from the central bank if there is one, or simply by printing notes. The rate of interest implied is zero in the case of printing notes, and for central bank loans it is probably very low. There are, however, usually fairly stringent conditions written into the constitutions of central banks, concerning the length of loans, and perhaps also the total amount which they can legally advance to the government. The economic effect of deficit finance is to transfer command over economic resources to those receiving the new money, leading (directly and indirectly) through their increased spending to a pressure on goods and services, and probably to some degree of price rise. This is at the expense of those whose incomes have not risen, who find that they cannot purchase all they could previously afford. They will consequently be driven into involuntary or forced saving. The expectation is that those receiving the command over resources will make more productive use of them than those who are deprived.

In principle this process operates to some extent in any economy. It is even probable that in most circumstances a certain amount of new investment will result from the deficit finance, over and

1. cf. Shanti Lal Sarupia, *Economic Weekly*, 22 June, 1963.

2. cf. R. Galletti *et al.*, *Nigerian Cocoa Farmers*, Oxford, 1956.

3. There appear to be two meanings of the term 'deficit finance' in circulation. In the advanced countries it normally implies that the current budget is not balanced out of current resources. It is assumed that it can easily be covered by borrowing, probably on short term, from commercial banks or other financial institutions or from the general public. In India, and perhaps in other development countries, the term deficit finance applies only to borrowing from the Reserve Bank after other forms of loan finance have been exhausted. From the point of view of the sequence of economic effects the difference in interpretation is usually not very important.

above what would have taken place in its absence. The effect on the real national income, however, is likely to be much weaker in a development country than in an industrialised one. In the latter deficit finance is appropriate in a situation in which there are resources of labour and equipment standing idle, which will immediately be turned to productive use as a result of the new demand. In a development country, even in one that is suffering from population pressure, there is much less scope for this sequence of events. Unlimited population, even of working age, is (as we have seen) not synonymous in most development countries with a surplus productive labour force. Indeed there is often an acute shortage of competent factory workers. Nor is there likely to be a large reserve of idle equipment with which any surplus labour could co-operate.[1]

In the normal course of events the development process exhibits three distinct phases. The first phase is dominated by the construction of fixed capital—and all that that implies in co-operating factors. This phase is very costly, so that the strain on prices is severe. In the second phase the hope is that the redistribution of income that will have occurred may generate sufficient savings to prevent prices boiling over or the balance of payments collapsing. In the third phase, when the additional consumers' goods come on the market, prices should flatten out and may actually fall. The worst strain will have been mastered. Unfortunately this happy train of events is not very likely to be fully realised, since the tempo of development expenditure should go on increasing for a long period. It is clear, however, that a forcing of investment by deficit finance will make the first, most dangerous phase more difficult to weather—although at the same time it may accelerate the process of development and so shorten the period of strain.

At this point a variety of factors have to be taken into consideration, and their relative importance carefully weighed by the planners. The type of construction being undertaken is of first importance, including the speed and efficiency of its implementation, so that productive operation may be secured as soon as possible. (This suggests that, especially in the early stages of development, large and complicated works should be avoided.)[2]

---

1. On all this subject the analysis in Sir Arthur Lewis' *The Theory of Economic Growth*, Allen and Unwin, 1959, is particularly useful.
2. India would have spared herself much agony if she had not tried to build so many steel works at once.

Very important differences in the economic sequence depend on who gets the additional incomes (inflationary profits) at the second round. In a country where entrepreneurship is scarce increased output in the private sector will be small. Merchants and importers, however, are likely to be quickly off the mark with increased imports of consumers' goods. The effect on the balance of payments may therefore be very serious, and if an attempt is made to deal with it by import controls the rise in prices will be exaggerated.

Fundamental to the effects are the propensity to consume out of marginal income on the one side and the elasticity of supply of consumers' goods on the other. The latter depends very largely on the richness of natural resources that can be tapped. If the balance of payments is sufficiently strong the situation can be relieved by imports. It appears that the natural marginal propensity to consume differs substantially from one development country to another. (It is typically high in the West Indies and low in India.) There are no doubt multiple causes of these differences, such as the demonstration effect of neighbouring rich countries, or tourists, on the one hand, and a long tradition of poverty and want in the other direction. The Ghandian philosophy has also served India well by keeping down the spending of the richer elements in the country. Habits of spending may, however, change very quickly (it may be that this is already happening in India), and it is the business of the local statisticians to keep a close watch on them. The effect of aggressive trade unions should also be borne in mind. A demand inflation may all too easily turn into a cost inflation, leading to the well known spiral.

From these considerations it emerges that some countries can stand a great deal more deficit finance than others. A government that has over-indulged can seek to bring the situation back into control along three routes: (1) by price and import controls; (ii) by tightening commercial bank credit; and (iii) by high marginal tax rates. We shall deal with the last of these in the next chapter. The second implies the existence of a central bank with effective control over the commercial banks, and we shall examine it below. A word, however, must be said on the possibility of price controls.

It is argued by some economists that control of a few key prices will be sufficient to prevent a cumulative rise. This policy could only be effective if it were accompanied by rationing. But the situation is not likely to be one where this would be tolerated, even if it could be successfully administered (which is far from certain). Hence the effort to control prices could only have extremely arbitrary, and in some cases very cruel, effects.

The experience of India in this respect is particularly illuminating. During the implementation of the Second Plan, although a few key prices were controlled, the balance of payments collapsed as a result of a rapid increase of imports of a wide range of consumers' goods. As a consequence the implementation of the Plan was seriously delayed. For the Third Plan, in addition, a very tight control of imports of consumer's goods was imposed. By that time, however, Indian substitutes of some sort were available for most of the things that people wanted to buy. The main result of the control of imports was consequently a loss of potential exports.[1] It may be concluded that in a country such as India where there is a substantial sector of middle incomes with well developed demand schedules, price control would only stem a price rise at very great administrative cost, even if it were possible to implement it.

We must therefore examine the available means of using financial policy to increase savings and so contain the pressure on prices. There can be no doubt concerning the need for additional savings in development countries. Voluntary savings may well be a more important means than taxation of transferring command over resources to development so far as public investment is concerned, since savings from current budget surpluses are not likely to be large. In respect of private investment additional savings are vital. In an advanced country depreciation quotas on existing equipment will probably supply most of what is required for new investment automatically, without calling for conscious additional effort. In a development country there can only be a very meagre flow of funds from existing installations, and conscious effort is imperative.

5. Building the Financial Infrastructure

The answer to the problem of increasing home savings and harnessing them to development lies in creating an effective financial infrastructure.[2] This is not something that the development countries can afford just to let grow, as it did in England and

1. cf. I. M. D. Little, 'A Critical Examination of India's Third Five Year Plan', *Oxford Economic Papers*, 14, 1962, 1.
2. cf. on all this E. T. Nevin, *Capital Funds in Underdeveloped Countries*, Macmillan, 1961.

the U.S.A.; they have not time to wait for this to happen. Nor is it necessary that they should do so; there has been enough experimentation and accumulated knowledge to lay down with fair confidence both what is required and what is feasible. Broadly, a financial infrastructure comprises four elements, each of which can become a source of additional savings. These four elements are, first, the currency, secondly a central bank, thirdly an effective commercial banking system (including savings institutions), and fourthly a foundation for the growth of developed monetary institutions, including a market for short term funds and a stock exchange.

The establishment of an adequate financial infrastructure inevitably takes time. But it will take less time and be more effective if it is undertaken as a deliberate and integrated policy. In some countries primitive habits of investment—in cattle, regardless of quality, or in gold and jewelry—have to be overcome before savings can be made available for development. Again some development countries had central banks during the interwar period. Their experience over the years should be useful in respect of such things as forecasting seasonal movements. In other directions, however, it may not be of much present relevance. In the interwar period banking operations were carried on in a world where there was no conscious push for development. The central banks' preoccupations were with primary product prices, the objective being international stability rather than growth. Relations between the central bank and the government tended to be much less intimate than is required in a development country. Thus, even where a country possesses an established central bank, its outlook and possibly also its constitution will require adjustment to the idea that its main task must be to support development policy.

The most obvious source of funds that can be mobilised for development is the unnecessarily large reserves with which many countries emerged into independence, particularly those countries where Currency Boards had been in operation. The essence of the Currency Board system is that its operation is virtually automatic. The supply of currency in a country depends on the flow of foreign exchange into and out of it. An outflow automatically reduces the money supply (credit money being of negligible importance); a favourable balance of payments has the opposite effect. Thus there is absolute security against a balance of payments crisis, but none against violent income changes within the country. Traditionally sterling Currency Boards operated with 100 per cent backing; but since 1954 the Bank of England has agreed that 80 per cent provides sufficient cover in most circumstances. This has constituted a welcome, although once for all, addition to development funds. What has now taken place is the change over to an exchange standard, based, so far as Commonwealth countries are concerned, on sterling. (But since sterling is tied to the U.S. dollar, and the dollar to gold, the formal base is not of very great importance.)

The fundamental differences implied in this change is that an exchange standard requires a conscious monetary policy. The exchanges will fluctuate with all the economic winds that blow. The experience of one country will differ from another's according to such things as the natural strength of its balance of payments, and the extent to which its major exports fluctuate, both on the supply side (depending mainly on the vagaries of its climate) and on the demand side (depending on the extent to which they are tied to the level of activity in the advanced countries). A further factor is the extent to which the central bank will itself have to bear the whole burden of protecting the currency or to which overseas owned commercial banks will be prepared to lend a hand by offsetting fluctuations, for instance, by bringing in funds when a temporary outflow occurs.[1]

On the other side is the problem of keeping the internal money supply adjusted to social and economic change. For instance, as the subsistence sector comes into the money economy more currency will be required. On the other hand, the spread of banking habits will economise in currency, a tendency which the general limbering up of the economy will carry further through an increase in the velocity of circulation.

These are difficult matters which the monetary authorities will have to watch carefully, learning by experience to take the correct decisions. It will be advisable at the start to keep detailed records of currency issues and withdrawals, month by month. If it so happens that one particular foreign country is predominantly important to the development country in question, movements into and out of its exchange should be specially carefully watched. It may well be desirable to hold an ample reserve of its securities. Only experience will show what magnitude of reserves it is desirable for the bank to carry. It will almost certainly be substantially

---

1. If and when a country joins the International Monetary Fund a new world of advice and assistance (but perhaps subject to stringent conditions) will be open to it. It would take us too far afield to enter into a discussion of these relations.

lower than that required by even the modified Currency Board system; and a greater proportion of it can safely be held in local assets where it can directly assist development. (We shall return to this point below.)

In most countries the foreign exchange held as currency backing is by no means the only reserve that can be mobilised for development. Some primary producing countries, for instance, still have Marketing Board reserves invested overseas, but are reluctant to withdraw them, since, as they were invested when interest rates were very low, there would now be a substantial capital loss on realisation. These funds are now urgently needed for development, and there is no point in leaving them overseas, since interest rates are most unlikely to return to the low levels of the middle 1940's in the foreseeable future.

6. *Central Banking in Development Countries*

The main agency for the mobilisation of savings will be the central bank. Traditionally, as we have seen, the main objective of central bank policy was to preserve economic stability. Indeed (as in nineteenth-century England) when the public sector was still small, and consequently fiscal policy ineffective, the bank was the only stabilising agency. Stability is still an important objective of central bank policy; but in a development country, where the financial infrastructure is only in course of erection and where banking habits only touch a minor part of the economy, the contribution that a central bank can make to development is more important and immediate than what it can do in the way of stabilisation.

There is no difficulty in persuading development countries that they need a central bank, for it has become something of a prestige symbol. Once the true role of the bank is grasped it will be seen that it need not be a costly affair, with a magnificent building and an army of research officers (who would be better employed in the Planning Department). Hence even a small country can afford its own central bank, although it would be foolish to launch one if there were neighbouring territories with similar development interests with which it could join.[1] Generally speaking the larger

1. Thus there is no reason why the smaller Caribbean islands should not have their own central bank, apart from Jamaica or Trinidad, although a joint organisation with Trinidad would have greater opportunities. The similar economies of the East African countries (Kenya, Uganda, and Tanzania) suggest that they might co-operate in a central bank, even without formal federation. cf. W. T. Newlyn, Monetary Systems and Integration, E. A. Economic Review, June 1964.

the jurisdiction the greater and more regular the funds that the bank will have at its disposal, and so the greater the assistance it can give.

It is important, however, that the bank should be strong enough to wield a moral force that will command respect at home and inspire confidence abroad. Inclusion in the bank's statutes of provisions limiting the amount and length of loans to the government will help in this respect. For the sake of reassuring the established commercial banks it will also be well to announce that the central bank will not compete in commercial banking in any way. (It has been found by experience that the two functions do not go well together.) It will also help to inspire confidence if the bank establishes a separate 'Currency' Department, distinct from the Banking Department, the sole business of which would be to look after the soundness of the currency. In fact this provision has no compelling economic or financial rationale; but it follows the precedent of most well established and successful central banks.

Although the central bank's staff need not be large, it must be of the highest calibre. In a development country the bank will have to be set up almost wholly out of goverment funds, since no other source will be immediately available. This by no means implies that it should, or need, be the government's creature (or 'milch cow' as it is sometimes expressed). Its operations can, and should, be entirely unfettered. It should be in a position to give independent advice and to state its views firmly to the government, on the basis of its own economic and statistical research; although in the last analysis it will have to conform to the government's general economic policy. The idea current in the 1920's, when a number of central banks were set up, that central banks should be entirely independent of governments, has been realised to be impracticable in the face of the growth of public economic policy (dating from the depression of the 1930's[1]). On the other hand there is an important sense in which a well established central bank can never be 'nationalised'. Thus it can do much to maintain confidence among the business community at home and abroad, when governments act in a manner which is clearly not in the long run interests of the economy.

1. It can be argued that from the Bank Act of 1844 the Bank of England was not fully independent of the government, since it could not expand the currency to reflate a crisis without the authorisation of a 'Treasury Letter'.

What then should be the main function of a central bank in a development country? It will naturally be the government banker both on current and capital account, and will have responsibility for national debt transactions. Thus it will be in very close contact with the government's economic policy. By acting as a channel for savings from public reserves, and also from the general public's purchase of savings certificates and similar securities, it can directly aid the finance of development.[1]

The central bank will probably not be able to do very much to regulate the activities of foreign owned banks; but it can begin at once to require them to keep reserves with it, related (in some way) to their transactions in the country. (Professor Nevin[2] makes the useful point that these should be prescribed in terms of sums of money rather than in ratios, first because the appropriate ratios for such local transactions would be hard to determine, and secondly because a multiple credit expansion (or contraction) cannot be expected in the early stages of development. The crude quantity theory will operate much more nearly than in a developed credit economy.) Some of these bank reserves can safely be invested in development by the bank itself, as they are not likely to fluctuate very violently.

From the beginning the central bank must be given powers to change the reserve requirements of the commercial banks according to the needs of stability policy. The withdrawal of definite sums from circulation should have an immediate anti-inflationary effect on the economy. On the other side it should be given powers to encourage investment in particular lines by selective credit controls through the banks and through such financial institutions as insurance companies and building societies. In all these ways[3] the central bank can channel savings into the development process while doing what it can to see that stability is observed.

The central bank's second task will be to watch over the establishment of a sound commercial banking system throughout the

1. According to circumstances it may or may not be useful to set up a separate, 'Development Bank' to look after this channeling process. The alternative is for the central bank to operate directly through such agencies as an Industrial Development Corporation and an Agricultural Credit Corporation.

2. Op. cit.

3. It would take us too far into the field of technicalities to discuss the use of multiple exchange rates as a means of selective credit controls and export stimulators. Experience seems to indicate that they are mainly of use as short run devices when the situation has got too involved for more orthodox methods to be successful.

country. Long established branches of foreign owned banks have rendered a very useful service in promoting overseas trade and in establishing a tradition of sound banking. But they have normally taken more out of these countries than they have put in. Some few of these banks are now prepared to re-orientate their policy and to take an active part in providing credit for development; but this does not seem to be general.

The central bank may consequently find that it has to build up an internal banking structure almost from the bottom. One way of doing this is to establish a commercial bank with public funds, which will follow an aggressive policy of 'selling' banking even in remote rural areas.[1] In some countries private enterprise is willing to come forward and set up local branch banking. It will be the central bank's responsibility to see that adequate legislation is ready in advance to look after these.[2] The legislation should stipulate such things as the minimum subscribed capital, the minimum ratio of deposits to capital, acceptable qualifications for directors, and the assets which the bank is permitted (or forbidden) to hold. Even if the promotors are sound and solid men (which by no means follows), they will be very inexperienced in financial matters and will need both protection and guidance in the early years.

In respect of old established banks, whether foreign owned or not, the central bank will be wise to proceed very tactfully. They have to be convinced that in the long run the setting up of the central bank will be to their advantage. In fact this is true[3] in several ways. Its existence will directly enlarge the field in which they can operate. It can simplify transactions by giving assistance with clearings and other services. The establishment of financial markets, especially a money market, will be a great convenience to the banks as a means of investing short term balances. On the other hand the central bank would be wise not to force too high a block of reserves to be held locally. The objective should be not to hinder the banks in their business but to lead them into either holding cash (which would help to restrain inflationary pressures), or, better, to activate them to look for new forms of productive investment.

1. This was successful in Ceylon.
2. As was not the case in Nigeria, though no fault of the government.
3. In Canada in the 1920's an international recommendation that a central bank should be established was greeted with scant favour by the well established and responsible commercial banks. It was not long before they discovered the advantages of having one. cf. A. F. W. Plumptre, *Central Banking in the British Dominions*, Toronto, 1947.

The established banks will also be grateful to find that the central bank's control over inexperienced bankers will protect them from bad banking.

In an advanced country the commercial banks are far from being the only sources of credit or depositories for savings. Over the years many other institutions, such as insurance companies and building societies, have developed spontaneously. In a development country such institutions are needed here and now, and so must be deliberately created. In a development country lending risks are so high that without the intermediary of government backed agencies savings will either tend not to be made, or will merely be hoarded. The answer to this is a government organisation or savings banks and savings certificates.[1] The central bank can offer invaluable advice on the lending policy of the agencies. The way in which it will be convenient to organise them, however, depends very much on the types of credit demand in the country. The provision of credit for private enterprise is vital to development. It is important to realise that the problem breaks down into three separate compartments: credit for (relatively) large scale enterprise, credit for agriculture, and credit for small business.

Industrial and hotel credit (representing large business) should be on a strictly commercial basis. It would naturally be handled by an Industrial Development Corporation and a Tourist Board, respectively. It would be their responsibility to make the necessary enquiries into the antecedents of the applicants and into their capital position. These agencies would naturally work closely with the Revenue Department operating the tax concession legislation.

Credit for agriculture (other than plantations), and for small scale enterprise, is on a different footing. It has to be recognised that it is partly a social service in which an element of subsidy will be necessary. In respect of agriculture the administration of credit can usefully be combined with other agricultural services and advisory organisations. If producers' co-operatives can be effectively organised for particular products (especially for tree crops where continuity of tenure can be taken for granted), credit can most conveniently be organised on the advice of the primary societies. In respect of credit for the little man there is considerable danger (as we saw in the last chapter) that a government may entangle itself in bad debts and open-ended subsidies which

---

1. Japan has been remarkably successful in the mobilisation of small savings, considering her poverty. India has also done creditably.

contribute little to development. It is consequently important that the conditions under which credit will be given should carefully be laid down and that the administration of grants and collection of interest should be strictly regular and without political favour. The actual terms can then be generous.

The final task of a central bank in building the financial infrastructure should be to lay the foundations of markets for short and long term securities.[1] In this exercise there must clearly be very close co-operation between the bank and the government. The bank can help as regards the short term market by accepting and encouraging the use of familiar types of credit, not excluding bills of lading. But the best stock in trade for the market will be Treasury Bills. The bank should encourage the government to make regular, fairly uniform, short term issues of these, at reasonably attractive (tender) rates and carrying re-discount facilities. The objective is not so much the convenience of the government as the convenience of investors: 'to establish a regular and acceptable channel by which private investors may obtain suitable assets within the economy, and local enterprises may obtain access to funds which would otherwise be lost to investment within the country.'[2]

Some development countries have already long established stock exchanges, but for those who have not the nucleus of a market in long term loans will be, to start with (and perhaps for a considerable time), trading in government debt. For success in this field again, the wishes of investors rather than the special interests of the government should have the first claim. The government can arrange its borrowing so that loans are issued fairly frequently and regularly. They should be planned to have the widest possible appeal to private investors, not merely to the banks and insurance companies. Experience shows that government debt is a perfectly good foundation for security trading.[3] In a development country the central bank can co-operate in the establishment of a stock exchange, for instance by organising (perhaps to start with on the bank's premises) weekly meetings of those interested in buying and selling government debt. Besides arranging its borrowing with a

1. 'The encouragement of rudimentary markets in long and short term loans is a task of first importance.' (Nevin, op. cit., p. 85.)

2. Nevin, op. cit., p. 95.

3. In pre-1914 England, apart from the railways, almost the whole of the home stock in trade of the London Stock Exchange was Government debt.

view to the interests of investors, the government can help by giving sufficient support to bond prices to prevent wide fluctuations.

Building up an effective central bank, and still more establishing a complete financial infrastructure, are long term operations and patience is necessary. Nevertheless in some development countries where structures of a new type have been set up (for instance Jamaica and Nigeria), considerable progress has been made even within a few years. As money and credit institutions develop, monetary policy will become increasingly available to assist fiscal policy to make the course of development as smooth and as rapid as the resources of the country will allow. Nevertheless in most development countries today, and for the immediate future, fiscal policy will continue to be the senior partner. To its consideration we must consequently turn.

CHAPTER FOUR

FISCAL POLICY FOR DEVELOPMENT: TAXES ON OUTGOINGS

1. *The Instruments of Policy*

FISCAL policy may be taken to embrace all government transactions which have as their objective the support of general economic policy. In an advanced country (at least of the welfare state type) general economic, as distinct from political, policy, is geared to promote growth with stability and to increase welfare through a more equal distribution of available (spendable) incomes. In an advanced country fiscal policy very largely operates on the expenditure side of the account, through widespread social expenditure and through selective incentives directed to particular industries or localities which it is desired to encourage. These are both long term fields of operation. Expenditure policy is also extremely important in respect of short term stability (compensatory finance), because of the ease with which alterations can be brought about in social expenditure, or, more precisely, in the balance between social expenditure and social taxation (insurance contributions).

Main reliance for income redistribution falls, however, on the tax side of the account. By controlling the available incomes of the rich and by redistributing capital assets through taxation a far greater equality of spending power is obtained than results from the productive process. Increasingly also, on the side of production, attempts are made to write into tax formulae (especially of profits taxes) incentives for investment, both general and selective. These too can be varied over time in the interests of stability.

Thus fiscal policy in an advanced country comprises a large armoury of weapons, some concentrating mainly on welfare effects, others on considerations of economic growth with stability; some aiming mainly at short term effects, others at long term development. By no means all these objectives are consistent. For instance redistribution carried out too violently, or a stability policy which reaches the point of long term disincentive, are both inimical to growth. Subsidies to certain industries (particularly to agriculture, which are the most general) may counteract an income redistribution policy by forcing consumers to pay more for their food, thus injuring the poor more than the rich.

In a development country the main emphasis of general economic policy will be on growth, with sufficient stability to prevent recurrent crises which would cause development to slow up or even retrogress, and hence give rise to losses on investments already made. With different emphasis in different countries, it will probably also be desired to use fiscal policy to reduce the very large gap between the incomes of the few rich and many poor which we found to be typical of development countries. On the expenditure side there is not likely to be a great deal of opportunity for a policy either of income redistribution through social expenditure or of stabilisation through compensatory variations in public outlay (though the means for this must be explored). In all lines of expenditure growth must have the priority. Hence the heaviest responsibility both for stability and for income redistribution must fall on the tax side of the account.

In the last chapter we examined the means of finance available for development, other than current internal receipts (of which by far the most important is taxation). Although we found that these other opportunities of finance offered a wide potential range, either they were quantitatively not very important (sources derived from domestic savings), or else (foreign aid) they could not be used very liberally without giving rise to subsequent troubles. Taxation is thus by far the most important source of development finance, both for the direct contribution which it can make, and for its indirect effects on control and on incentive and in narrowing the gap in available incomes. It is consequently most important that tax policy in development countries should be strong. Unfortunately it is almost invariably a weak and unreliable weapon in their armouries.[1] As we have seen, the ratio of tax revenue to G.N.P. in the advanced countries is normally of the order of at least 30 per cent, allowing for the collections of all levels of government. In the development countries it is rarely much more than half that. In some development countries it is even now less than 12 per cent. Moreover, the higher percentages often reflect a high

---

1. Frustrated by giving repeated advice on this head which proved ineffective, Mr. N. Kaldor once wrote: 'Will the underdeveloped countries never learn to collect taxes?' cf. *Foreign Affairs*, 1962.

revenue from export taxes imposed on expatriate firms, a policy which, as we shall see, is not fully effective for what should be the tax purposes of development countries.

Our task in this and the following chapter will be to investigate the means of improving this situation. It can be approached along two lines: first, the choice of the most appropriate taxes for development, and secondly, devices for assessing and collecting them to better standards than hitherto. Before we begin our tax study however we should take a brief glance at other possible sources of current revenue. In as much as these could also provide a useful source of finance they would relieve the pressure on taxes. The view that this is possible is widely held, for instance in municipal circles in India. It cannot be denied that some governments, especially at the local level, have made a considerable success of municipal trading services. This has not infrequently been because (as in Australia) they have been denied access to normal taxes, so that trading profits have been their best hope of autonomous revenue. This experience, however, does not prove that a large untapped source of development finance could be made available either along these lines, or from other forms of current incomings.

The possible sources of current receipts other than taxes (and apart from such casual incomings as court fees and fines), are, first, interest on past loans; secondly, rent on houses and other buildings owned by the government; thirdly, licences; and fourthly profits of publicly owned commercial undertakings. A mere listing of these suggests that they are not likely to be important in a developing country. National governments indeed may receive interest on loans made to local authorities, but in the national accounts this constitutes no additional item. They may also to some limited extent receive interest on loans to individuals, for instance for agricultural development or small business; but these are likely to accrue to the Agricultural Credit Corporation or the Industrial Development Corporation, which will want to use them as a revolving fund, so that they are not generally available for development purposes.

Some governments provide housing for their employees for which they charge a rent, but this is usually highly subsidised and should be regarded as an alternative to paying higher salaries. Loans for car purchase fall into the same category. The primary purpose of licences is regulatory: in respect of practising certain trades or carrying on particular occupations. It would clearly be wrong to charge so much for the licences in the interests of the budget as to prevent the operation of the licensed activities. Radio and television licences are in a different class. It is highly desirable that these amenities should be available as widely as possible, especially in rural areas, for agricultural and general educational purposes. Motor vehicle licences are again somewhat different. They do have a regulatory aspect, but by and large they are a form of tax, and an increasingly lucrative one. We shall return to them in relation to other means of taxing motoring.

Profits of publicly owned commercial undertakings may for present purposes be divided into three categories. First, government monopolies of the manufacture of certain products, especially such things as tobacco, salt or matches. These are intended as an alternative to taxes. Secondly, manufacturing industry similar to that conducted by private enterprise. Thirdly, public utilities, many of which are natural monopolies (in the sense that more than one undertaking cannot sensibly operate in an area).

State monopolies as a substitute for taxes are much favoured in continental European countries, and in those development countries which follow their pattern. There appear to be no advantages and some disadvantages in extracting revenue from consumers in this way rather than by straight taxes. The public authorities have all the trouble of running a business, for which they are probably not very well suited, while consumers tend to suffer by a restriction on the varieties of the product which they can purchase (for instance cigarettes or matches). There is no evidence that from the revenue point of view the monopoly is more lucrative than taxes imposed on the same products would be.

It is difficult to generalise concerning profits from manufacturing industry. In an advanced country like France where there is an abundance of entrepreneurial ability, public ownership may be at least as efficient and profitable as private (witness the Renault motor works). In developing countries, however, entrepreneurial ability tends to be scarce. Indeed this is the reason which often tempts governments to undertake direct manufacturing; but there is no evidence that government finds it any easier than private enterprise to find the right sort of managers.[1] Moreover, a substantial range of public manufactures, such as drugs and fertilisers, are products which the government wishes to have available in

---

1. cf. a variety of Indian experience, H. K. Paranjape, *The Industrial Management Pool*, Indian Institute of Public Administration, 1962.

large supply and intends to sell at subsidised prices. These are a source of public outlay rather than of income.

The main publicly owned transport undertakings are the railways; but lucky is the country which can today even balance its railway budget, let alone make a profit. A profit can indeed be forced (as has been done in Japan and to some extent in East Africa for instance), by deliberately neglecting the roads; but this is not good economics. Bus services, especially in urban areas, are a more hopeful proposition. Under private enterprise they are often profitable; under public ownership they will probably be expected to serve other ends in addition to purely economic considerations. This all adds to costs. It would take us too far afield to discuss the diverse reasons why state enterprise either at the national or local level is not often a success in development countries in the economic sense. Our direct concern with the matter is merely that, as a source of revenue, it tends to be negligible.

It remains to discuss the commonest form of state enterprise of all: the public utility with a natural monopoly. Most of these enterprises have the characteristic that their capital costs are high and running costs very low; consequently unit costs tend to fall more and more as output expands. Since the state has a complete monopoly there is no fiscal reason why charges should not be high enough to realise a substantial net revenue. There, is however, a very good economic argument for keeping charges low, so that expanding demand can encourage operation at the cheapest possible level, consistent with covering the whole cost of the undertaking in the charges levied. If overheads are not covered in the pricing system they will have to be charged against general taxation. Too often this results in those who cannot enjoy the service subsidising those who do. This probably implies that rural areas which do not have the advantage of such services as water and electricity subsidise the urban areas which are, generally speaking, better off. Thus if the proper economic pricing policy is followed there is no hidden source of revenue available even here. We are consequently driven back on to the tax system as the chief and almost the only efficient source of current internal receipts for development finance.

2. Taxation for development: the basic needs

The first problem that we have to enquire into is the reason for the poor achievement of tax systems in development countries.

It is of course true that very big taxes cannot be raised from very poor people. But when we see countries at approximately the same level of development and with about the same per capita income, raising very different per capita revenue, it is clear that this is not an adequate explanation. In fact three major explanations can be advanced. First, and most fundamental, for a govermnent to assess and collect revenue efficiently and promptly it is essential that it should have the confidence of the citizens, in the sense both that the mass of potential taxpayers agree with its policies, and that they believe that it is sufficiently stable and united to carry out its declared intentions. In the absence of this confidence taxpayers are unlikely to comply unless or until they are forced to do so. At the best there will be frequent delays in collection: at the worst there will be widespread defaults. History is full of examples of governments which collapsed because they became unable to collect taxes.

Secondly, the officers to whom tax assessment and collection is entrusted must be intelligent, well trained in their jobs and incorruptible. It is essential that they be sufficiently well paid that there is no irresistible temptation on them to collect something on the side. This applies at all grades: the clerical (assessment) level and the higher inspectorate and administrative cadres also. This is a matter to which we shall return in the next chapter, in connection with income and profits taxes.

In addition to these well known weaknesses of tax administrations in development countries, there is another which is often overlooked, but which can be extremely important especially in relation to business profits taxes: the poor drafting of tax laws. The most expert officers in the world cannot collect tax adequately under laws that are riddled with loopholes and ambiguities. It is safe to say that no country, however advanced and experienced, is completely successful in drafting tax laws which are at one and the same time simple enough to be understood and yet capable of unambiguous interpretation. In respect of the taxation of high personal income and business profits the legal draftsmen are up against some of the best brains in the country. In most advanced countries an endless skirmishing persists between the revenue authorities on the one side and tax lawyers and company accountants on the other, as loophole after unsuspected loophole is stopped up. In the laws of development countries opportunities for avoidance are enormously greater. This can often be traced to the habit of incorporating long passages from the laws of other countries into the local laws, without understanding of the conditions which they were intended to meet in the first country.[1] There is no easy answer to this problem: but it is one to which the governments of development countries should be continually alert. In doubtful cases the opinion of the courts should be sought, and legislation immediately amended to remedy any defects discovered.

Before we discuss in detail the most appropriate taxes for development we must ask ourselves what precise contribution we expect taxes to make to the development process. We can distinguish at least five, most of which have already been touched on in passing. In the first place, in a development country taxes are the most efficient way of securing the transfer of command over resources to the government. Secondly, since private saving cannot be expected to go a long way, they need to be backed up by 'public saving'—precisely this transfer from the private to the public sector. Some economists assert that a national government has no need to tax in order to finance its outgoings, since it can always borrow internally. Hence the main purpose of taxation is to prevent inflation. This analysis is misleading in application to a development country, where (as we have seen) the opportunities for internal borrowing are very limited. It is of course not claimed that even in an advanced country, inflationary pressure would not develop very soon if an attempt were made to finance all outgoings by borrowing.

A third objective of taxation in a development country is to narrow the gap between the available incomes of the very rich and very poor. In principle it is easier to do this by taxation than any other way; but (as we shall discuss later) the adequate taxation of the rich calls for special care and expertise. Fourthly, taxes can contribute in several ways to encouraging economic instincts. They can give backward peoples an incentive to come out of their isolation and see for themselves things that money can buy and what development can do for them. We shall argue in the next chapter that a personal tax within their capacity to earn, spent on

1. The most striking example of this weakness that I have come across was the case of the U.N. official with no fiscal expertise whatever who was required to draft an income tax law for Libya. He sat down (metaphorically) with scissors and paste and incorporated at random passages from a large number of advanced country laws. Fortunately the result was so unintelligible that no one attempted to make any use of it. In justice to the U.N. it should be recorded that this episode belongs to the early postwar years.

public goods which directly improve their position, is an excellent way of doing this. At a higher income level a parallel effect can be obtained by a judiciously composed tax formula which will tempt both nationals and expatriates into the adventure of entrepeneurship, encouraging the establishment of new industries and the enlargement of existing factories. A by no means very favourable investigator[1] of Puerto Rico's 'Operation Bootstrap'[2] emphasises the beneficent effect of incentive tax concessions as a stimulus to the establishment of new industries, even although the main effect was psychological. This is a question which we shall be examining in the next chapter.

Finally, taxes are the most important instrument available in development countries for controlling the pressure on consumers' goods engendered by the development process, by draining off sufficient of the additional incomes to bring the total into equilibrium with the available supply of consumers' goods—of course after making allowance for the contribution of voluntary saving to the draining off process. This tax function is the special responsibility of the national government, because it calls for a careful and integrated choice from a wide range of taxes, so that the net result will be to steer a smooth course between the storms of inflation on the one side and uneasy calms of disincentive effect on the other. Moreover stability in this sense is (as we have seen) far from being a matter confined to internal tax policy. It is closely bound up with international trade policy, also a national government responsibility. It is most necessary for the national government to keep a watchful eye on tax revenue accruing from internationally traded goods, since the first symptoms of incipient inflation frequently show up in a sudden turn for the worse in the exchanges, caused by an abnormal increase in imports. Further, it will be the responsibility of the national government, in conjunction with the central bank, to gauge the increasing support which monetary and credit control can afford, and to adjust the tax structure accordingly.

Of this varied list of contributions which taxes can make to the development process the transfer of resources to the government and the balance of supply and demand in the national accounts are by far the most important, and must largely guide the choice of

---

1. M. C. Taylor, *Industrial Tax Concession in Puerto Rico*, University of Michigan, 1955.
2. See above, p. 38.

taxes. For the tax structure to perform these functions (especially the last), two conditions are necessary. In the first place revenue as a percentage of the national product must be sufficiently large to influence the level of economic activity in general, and that of consumption in particular. This probably implies that revenue should reach about 20 per cent. of the G.N.P. (Even this is not much more than half that expected in many advanced countries.) It is not possible to be dogmatic as to the ratio required, since the extent of control which a given revenue will exercise depends not only on its size, but also on the tax structure from which it is derived. On this ground alone a determined effort to increase the tax revenue is called for.

Secondly, so far as possible, taxes should be chosen such that as incomes rise the government will automatically secure an increasing proportion of them as revenue. That is to say, incremental tax incidence must be higher than average tax incidence. The obvious answer to this in principle is a progressive personal income tax: but this is not an easy tax to make effective. (We shall discuss ways of doing so in the next chapter.) Hence recourse will have to be made to other taxes which have something of the same effect. There is an obvious convenience in taxes which automatically increase their severity as incomes rise, since no politically awkward decisions are required. (It may naturally also be necessary to raise tax rates as the momentum of development expenditure increases.) If these two conditions are fulfilled a government should always be able to keep the situation in hand, because revenue will rise more rapidly than incomes.

For present purposes we can simply divide taxes into two classes: taxes on outgoings or outlay,[1] and taxes on incomings. This distinction corresponds broadly to the familiar British classification between indirect and direct taxes, but since this is an administrative and not an economic classification the correspondence is not complete.[2] In the present chapter we shall only be concerned with taxes on outgoings. It must be emphasised, however, from the start that our basic interest is in the effective (not the formal)

---

1. Since Mr. Kaldor used the term Expenditure Tax to describe a global tax progressive with all expenditure (effectively an income tax which exempts savings), it is better to use the terms outgoings or outlay for taxes on particular lines of spending; cf. N. Kaldor, *An Expenditure Law*, Allen and Unwin, 1955.

2. cf. U. K. Hicks, 'The Terminology of Tax Analysis', in *Readings in the Theory of Taxation*, ed. Shoup and Musgrave, American Economic Association, published by R. D. Irwin, 1959.

incidence of taxes.[1] We have to consider the entire change in the economic scene, including both income redistribution and reallocation of resources, brought about as a consequence of tax change. As an example, by collecting statistics of smokers, grouped in their income brackets (as the big tobacco companies frequently do), we can estimate the formal incidence of the revenue collected during a particular period in the sense of what income they parted with as they bought their cigarettes. But we need in addition to ask what action smokers took when the tax rate was changed, and what effect this had on the rest of their spending and saving; and in turn also what effects their changed propensities had on the organisation of the productive processes which found themselves disturbed.

It should also be emphasised that the revenue that matters is revenue *net* of the cost of collection. The cost of collecting income and profit taxes will inevitably be high while efficient departments are being set up, but this is a necessary expense and is only transitional. In advanced countries these are some of the cheapest taxes to administer per £ of revenue collected. More serious is the fact that in respect of a number of taxes on outgoings the full costs of collection are often concealed by faulty accounting, or by failing to take into account the time spent on tax collection by officers whose main work lies in other fields, such as agricultural officers who also collect produce taxes.

3. *Taxes on Outlay: Import Duties*

In a development country taxes on outgoings are very much more important as revenue raisers than in advanced countries. This largely reflects the difficulties of—and too often the want of serious effort put into—collecting taxes on incomings. In a typical development country taxes on outgoings may represent about 90 per cent of the revenue (unless taxes on incomings happen to be supported by heavy export taxes on primary products). In an advanced country the two categories of taxes bring in roughly the same amount of revenue, with, for instance in the U.K. and U.S.A., taxes on incomings slightly leading. The main types of taxes on outgoings are: (i) import duties; (ii) excise duties on home manufactures; (iii) sales and other related taxes; and (iv) taxes on the

1. U. K. Hicks, 'The Terminology of Tax Analysis', and *Public Finance*, Cambridge Economic Handbooks, 1955.

services or use of certain capital goods, typically motor cars and houses. Of these four categories import duties tend to be by far the most important, and typically account for about 30 per cent. of the tax revenue, while in advanced countries it is rare for import duties in the strict sense to amount to much more than about 10 per cent.

It must be remembered that all taxes on outgoings are more or less regressive against income: they take a larger percentage from small than from large incomes. This implies that they do not naturally fulfil the criterion of narrowing the income gap: in fact they tend to be anti-redistributional. But if these taxes are confined to luxury or semi-luxury goods which will only be purchased by the relatively wealthy, this may not matter so much. On the other hand, if a tax is to be useful as a controller of consumption it must have a broad base. For this purpose it is better to choose an article of mass consumption (such as salt or kerosene), but to keep the rates very low, so that although most people contribute, the burden even on poor families will only be a small one.[1]

One argument in favour of import duties is their ease of collection. No such great expertise is required of customs officials as it is of income tax assessors, merely honesty and a certain facility in simple arithmetic. Economically in development countries import duties are fairly satisfactory from the distributional point of view, because imported goods largely consist of luxuries or semi-luxuries consumed by townspeople whose incomes are higher, and will probably be increasing faster, than those of country dwellers. For this reason the tax extracted on the increment of income may well be higher than the tax on the average of income, so that they come within reasonable distance of satisfying this criterion also. In particular, high rates can be imposed with impunity on durable consumers' goods, (not excluding motor cars) and also on prestige articles such as foreign liquor and cigarettes. There are, however, fairly serious limits to the expansion of import duty revenue.

In the first place a country which becomes a member of GATT may encounter difficulties in raising its import duty rates; for development countries this need not perhaps be taken too seriously.[2]

1. For further development of this argument see my *Public Finance*, cit. Ch. X.
2. In the face of the growth of regional pacts the future of GATT itself becomes somewhat obscure; cf. M. L. Hoffman, 'Can the GATT system survive'?, *Lloyds Bank Review*, July 1964.

Secondly, in view of the generally regressive nature of these taxes, while it is legitimate to tax luxuries heavily, it is desirable to exempt staple foods, work clothes and similar basic necessities, in so far as these have to be imported. In is also sensible to exempt what may be termed modest incentive goods: the things that people first want to buy as they get a little more money. A good example of such goods is the bicycle. This is not merely a consumers' good contributing importantly to the breaking down of isolation; with a bicycle it is easy to get to the shops and cinemas of the nearest town. It can also be considered a producers' good since it greatly facilitates the marketing of small surpluses, such as for instance cotton or rubber latex. In a similar class of semiproducers' goods we can include farm lanterns and even umbrellas, eagerly bought by rural workers in all tropical countries.

For similar reasons it is desirable to tax at very low rates, or preferably to exempt completely, investment goods such as raw materials and semi-manufactured goods which will be further processed. A good deal of farm and factory equipment also comes under this heading. In a country where the tourist industry is important there will be strong pressure to exempt a wide range of hotel furniture, furnishings and other equipment. These, however, are in a different category from industrial equipment because they are consumers' or near consumers' goods. Consequently the temptation to claim unjustifiable replacements will be strong, and the rules must be drawn tightly enough to prevent leakages into private consumption.

The main administrative problem in respect to import duties is that of preventing smuggling. This nuisance varies enormously with circumstances: according to the rates which it is desired to impose and the rates levied in neighbouring countries, and also according to whether neighbouring countries have articles to sell which are in very keen demand in the tariff imposing country. The nuisance is at its worst on the Caribbean islands, where neighbouring French and Dutch islands have free ports, and where the demands for easily smuggled goods such as liquor and tobacco is extremely high. The only general answer to the problem is not to attempt too high rates of tax, even though they may be desirable on economic grounds, and to establish an efficient preventive service, which moreover will be backed up by the police. Even this policy is difficult in the Caribbean in view of the free ports and the ease of access to the flat and indented shores of many of the islands.[1]

One of the most general reasons why import duties are desired is for the protection of (infant) home industries. While this desire rests on reasonably strong arguments, governments will do well to view demands for protection circumspectly. As suggested in the last chapter, governments will be wise to reject out of hand industrial suggestions that look from the start like lame ducks. A well chosen industry for whose products a genuine potential market exists should not require more than light protection for a short period. Firms will probably also be enjoying substantial concessions on profits taxes in their initial period. To deprive consumers of a better choice and cheaper goods for long periods, for the sake of protecting inefficiency, is neither good economics nor good welfare.

4. *Excises and Similar Levies*

In development countries where the range of home manufactures is narrow, it cannot be expected that the opportunities for excise duties will be wide; but in most countries among the first manufactures to be set up will be beer and cigarettes, and in fact in all countries, including the most advanced, these are the two best exciseable products. Probably few countries would be prepared to maintain that the taxation of tobacco is anti-social because of its regression.[2] Most governments will be prepared to tax heavily those goods the demand for which is inelastic; and they will be right to do so, since even after a sharp rise in taxes consumers will buy much the same as before, so that the disturbance to budgeting and production is minimal. Moreover, excises on tobacco and cigarettes are usually pleasingly easy to administer, because manufacture is concentrated in a few big firms from whom tax can be collected directly. There is, it is true, some danger of competition from inferior—and sometimes dangerous—home made goods: 'black tobacco' and illicitly brewed or distilled liquor. The way round this difficulty is the same as for smuggling: preventive measures (on which expense should not be spared), and experimentation to discover how high tax rates can safely be put.

1. cf. my Fiscal Report on the Eastern Caribbean.
2. As was claimed by a Turkish civil servant to whom I was lecturing. In the same way rum is claimed to be a basic necessity by West Indians.

As development progresses excise will become an increasingly useful source of revenue, both because the consumption of these staple amenities will expand, and because a wider range of home manufactures will become exciseable. Apprehension is sometimes expressed that import substitution will lead to a serious fall of revenue which cannot be made good in other ways. It would clearly be disincentive to force excises on infant industries the moment they are beginning to find their feet. Such a policy could have a disastrous effect on the willingness to venture in manufacturing. It is, however, very unlikely that import substitution in a few lines will lead to a general fall in import revenue. As development progresses the range of goods imported will continually expand. Better incomes imply a larger not a smaller demand for imported goods.

There are in addition other taxes that can be exploited and which are similar in their economic effects to excise duties; namely on the provision of services, on the one hand entertainments of various sorts and on the other (where conditions allow) tourism. It should be noted that tourist taxation is very successfully exploited by the main tourist countries of Western Europe: Italy and Spain. It should also be noted, however, that in these countries the tourist industry is very carefully controlled, inspected and graded, and tax adjusted accordingly. The visitor thus has a guarantee that he will get value for whatever type of accommodation he chooses, and consequently has little objection to paying tax. Broadly tourist taxes can be imposed in either of two forms: a fixed per capita sum per unit of service (meal or night's lodging), or a percentage on the bill. Generally the latter is preferable as it taxes more heavily those who by their indulgence show that they are capable of paying more. The fixed sum method has some advantages in simplicity of administration, but it discourages long stays, which are the most profitable. In order to get over this difficulty some areas allow a 'tax holiday' for a limited period after a certain number of payments.

5. *Sales and Turnover Taxes*

What weight it is desired to put on import and excise duties depends however to a considerable extent on policy in respect of sales and related taxes, to which we must now turn. Under this heading we can include sales and purchase taxes, as well as various forms of turnover taxes. There is no fundamental difference between a sales and a purchase tax (since every sale implies a purchase); but in common usage the term sales tax is applied to a low rate tax (5 per cent would be very high) imposed on a wide range of commodities, while a purchase tax denotes a selective tax imposed at high and probably differing rates on a limited range of goods. (At times some British purchase tax rates have actually reached 100 per cent.) Both taxes may have their uses. The broad base of the sales tax indicates it as an instrument for the control of mass consumption, but unless basic necessities are exempted its regression may become serious. The differing rates of purchase tax enable its regression to be mitigated by restricting the very high rates to luxury goods. Differing rates also permit of its use for the encouragement (discouragement) of the consumption of particular goods.

The rates of whichever tax is used clearly need to be integrated with rates currently imposed on imported goods. (There is little point in subjecting exciseable goods to purchase tax, since the excise rates can always be freely varied.) Import taxes are usually assessed on a specific basis (so much per unit of the commodity)[1] while sales or purchase taxes will have been assessed on an *ad valorem* basis (as a proportion of the cost including selling costs). If care is not taken the combined assessment may inadvertently come near to exclusion. (Even this is preferable from the trade point of view to the total exclusion which may be brought about by a manipulation of quotas.)

The possibility of near exclusion through a combination of import duties and sales taxes indicates, however, a useful line of policy in a balance of payments crisis. Sales tax rates can be freely moved up, although import duties cannot. For such a policy to succeed, however, the rates of both taxes need to be under the control of the national government. This will certainly be the case with import duties; but in federations (as we shall discuss in chapter VI) sales taxes have proved one of the most useful sources of autonomous revenue available to state governments. This is true both in a rich federation such as the U.S.A. and in a poor one such as India. If differences arise between national policy and state

---

1. For a development country this is the wiser course, due to the difficulties and delays entailed in determining the prices needed for *ad valorem* assessment. The only trouble about specific assessment is that as prices rise tax rates must be raised from time to time, so that the revenue in real terms does not diminish.

preferences in this respect, the national government may have to take powers to limit the autonomy of states in respect of sales tax rates to some extent. In fact this has already been done in India, as we shall see.

Although sales taxes bring in substantial revenue in development countries it is unlikely that anything like the full revenue due is collected anywhere. Consequently the question has to be faced as to whether a tolerable degree of equity in administering the tax can be obtained. If not it may be better to conclude that under present conditions of retailing general sales taxes should not be used.[1] Two major difficulties in administration have to be faced. In the first place the ubiquitous primitive selling by the roadside, and similar methods of retailing, can hardly be subjected to tax. Only those retailers who sell in shops or bazaars in a reasonably orderly manner can be brought within its purview. Retailers require to be individually registered, and then carefully checked to see that on the one hand they collect tax on what they sell, and on the other that when tax rates are raised they do not charge wildly higher prices than is justified by the rise in tax.

The second difficulty is that of the inspectorate. Can sufficient reliable inspectors be mustered to check the operation of the tax, remembering that selling points are very numerous and dispersed, not neatly gathered together in customs sheds or big factories? There is no general answer to these problems. It can be affirmed, however, that the chances of tolerable administration are better at the national than at any lower level of government. As regards coverage, the richer the community the greater the relative value of sales by retailers who can be registered, and hence the better coverage and equity of the tax. Thus Bombay state (or at least that part of it which is now in Maharashtra), is enthusiastic for sales tax,[2] while a poor state like Bihar does not derive much revenue and is not at all happy about it. In general judgment, however, the benefits of the sales tax in India substantially exceed its evils. So far as other development countries are concerned sales taxes should be regarded as a possible weapon in the armoury, rather than one for inevitable adoption.

This may be a convenient place to turn aside for a moment to

---

1. This was the view of the (Raisman) Fiscal Commission in Nigeria (Cmd 481 of 1958). Consequently they cannot be used in that country without fresh federal legislation.

2 1. See below, p. 122.

consider the place of the complex of taxes on motoring in a rational tax system for a development country, and the balance which should be preserved between the different methods of taxing. As we have seen, motoring can be taxed in four different ways: by import duties, licences, sales taxes and fuel taxes. The first three are related to the size or weight of the vehicle, the last to the degree of usage. The desirability of earmarking some of the revenue for road development should also be considered. In general in poor countries private motoring, especially in prestige cars, does not deserve any great encouragement and is a very legitimate subject for stiff taxation. In general it appears that development countries do not tax this amenity as highly as they should, partly no doubt because it tends to be viewed by Ministers as one of the major sweets of office.

The various motoring taxes are, however, capable of yielding a very substantial and rapidly increasing revenue. There is also the consideration that improved transport facilities are highly desirable in a development country for facilitating the movement of goods and people and breaking down isolationism. The answer would seem to be differential taxation in favour of motor bicycles and the cheaper forms of motoring, including lorries and buses. Differentiation can be applied very easily both by duties and by fuel taxes. It is often wise to tax the actual vehicles heavily, but to exempt or to tax very lightly spare parts and replacements, thus mitigating the incentive for thefts of car parts, which is a very serious nuisance in some countries. The policy of earmarking motor taxation for road development always tends to come up against the difficulty that the taxable capacity of motorists and the needs of road development do not necessarily run parallel. In general the selection of a tax and the selection of an expenditure are essentially two separate choices, each to be made on its merits. There is no reason why this argument should not apply to motoring as well as to other things. In a development country, moreover, there will surely be higher priorities for the use of a good block of revenue than applying the whole of it to the roads.

A turnover tax in the traditional sense is a low rate levy on the total value of sales of goods as they pass from firm to firm, and finally into consumption, in the processes of manufacturing and marketing. It is thus in essence a business tax, but in so far as firms add the tax to the selling prices of their products it operates as a very general sales tax, and can exert a strong control over consumption. From this angle it is an additional tax on consumption which neither requires customs control not gets into trouble with GATT. It appears that in practice firms do pass on most of the tax immediately. Unlike an income tax, liability is easily estimated in advance, and as the tax is frequently collected in monthly instalments, any errors in calculation of what the market will bear can be quickly corrected. Regarded as a tax on business, the turnover tax has the advantage over an income tax that there is no need to value new investment or depreciation, since the assessment makes no distinction between current and capital account. This indicates, however, that it is, compared to a tax on net profits, a crude and imprecise instrument.

The traditional turnover tax, as has been said, is assessed on the full value of sales, without deduction, at each transfer (this form is still used in Western Germany). This has two disadvantages. First the tax is 'pyramided' as the goods pass from firm to firm since at each stage the price charged includes the tax on that stage. Thus finally the consumer pays considerably more than the straight costs of production and marketing would warrant. Secondly the tax encourages the integration of productive processes within a single firm, as tax will thus be saved. This tends to discriminate against small firms and to discourage competition. In order to circumvent these disadvantages a more refined form of the tax is used in a number of countries (France was a pioneer in this respect). This is the Tax on Value Added (T.V.A.). At every stage tax is imposed not on total sales value but on sales *less* purchases from other firms. That is to say tax falls only on the 'value added' in the firm by the labour it employs, as it operates with the capital it owns, on the raw materials which it has bought. This is a decided improvement. The value added form has the further advantage in the ease with which exemption—drawback—can be granted on exported goods. Exemption can always be claimed at the final stage, but many countries award much more than this when they use the value added tax. (It is less easy to do this with the straight turnover tax.) In this respect also the T.V.A. is a way of getting round GATT as the goods are sold at a lower price, and hence at a larger profit abroad than at home. (It should be noted that exemption for exports can also be arranged under the British type Purchase Tax, but the range of goods eligible is very much narrower.) In so far, however, as home consumers are successfully charged the full increase in price when tax rises, profits on home sales should be just as good as on exports, so that there is no positive incentive to seek export markets.

The administration of these turnover taxes is extremely simple. Firms (unless they are of quite negligible size) are registered, irrespective of whether they are incorporated or not. They are then required to make a periodic return (say once a month) of the value of their sales, and to send it to the authorities together with vouchers recording purchases from other firms. Tax is assessed immediately on these returns, subject to whatever check the authorities like to use. Normally this is by a fairly small sample, with severe penalties for any false returns discovered. If desired the rates can differ from one line of production to another in much the same way as for British purchase tax. A tax of this nature might be a real advantage to a development country such as India which has an urgent need to export manufactured products. In development countries whose exports consist mainly of primary products traded on world markets, it would not seem to have much scope if applied to exports. On the other hand, as the range of home manufactured goods expands, it might prove more convenient to tax some of them in this way rather than by an excise.

It remains to discuss taxes on the services of durable goods. In practice net revenue from taxes on such services is derived from 'licences' on motor vehicles and taxes on the occupation of land and buildings. In the conditions of a development country neither of these taxes is heavily regressive. A certain accumulation of wealth is required before a motor car can be purchased; in practice very poor families cannot be brought within the scope of a house occupancy tax. As we have already discussed taxes on motoring we can proceed at once to the very important subject of the taxation of land and buildings. In the U.K. this tax is known as the 'rate' and is an autonomous (indeed the only autonomous) tax for local authorities.[1] It is a very powerful tax, exceeding in revenue all other taxes on outgoings, bringing in annually some £900 million. Unfortunately there are very few development countries which make anything like adequate use of this very useful levy.

---

1. The fact that the rate is under the jurisdiction of the local authorities in the U.K. has led to the mistaken idea that a national levy is a tax and a local levy a rate. The rate is so called because it takes the form of a flat rate tax levied on a predetermined valuation.

6. *A Tax (Rate) on Urban Land and Buildings*

Most countries make some use of a tax on land, which may include buildings; others tax buildings but leave the land untaxed. Most of these taxes are, however, assessed on the value (real or potential) of a particular form of property, and, generally speaking, the valuation is primitive and out of date. As the case of the U.K. shows, it is also possible for the tax to be levied on the occupier according to the annual rental value instead of on the property owner according to the (capital) value, and it is the former type which we shall consider in the present chapter; although in the next chapter we shall argue that, all things considered, the capital value base is probably more useful for development countries.[1] Many of the administrative problems are similar whichever form of tax is used. The rental form of tax is only sensible if a large range of property is in fact rented—and under such conditions that the tenants can be made subject to the tax. An annual value can be obtained from a capital value by using a suitable rate of interest as a reducer; but the choice of this can only be arbitrary, and the excercise is certainly not worth while.

We can discuss the practical problems concerning this tax— however operated—under three headings: valuation, assessment and collection. If, as is very likely, the tax is a local government responsibility, allowance must be made for relative inefficiency of local administrations; but by no means all the failures are due to this cause. Rather it is a reason why the national government should do everything it can to help, short of taking over assessment and collection or dictating the rate of tax. The first valuation problem is to determine the boundaries of holdings, no easy matter in a densely overcrowded tropical city. Next, 'fair' rents as a tax base have to be imputed wherever the actual rent paid is obviously out of line. For the first valuation it will pay a development country to hire the services of a team of professional valuers who are accustomed to this sort of exercise.

It is important that the same valuers should value the whole area, and that the valuations should be carried out as rapidly as possible, so that they should all have the same background price structure. It may well be desirable that the outside valuers should have available the advice of local leaders, for instance on matters

---

1. It will be apparent that a tax assessed on occupation is a tax on outgoings, whereas a tax on ownership is a tax on incomings.

of boundaries, and the government should see that this is forth-coming.[1] The government should also insist that local officers are chosen to learn the technique. The most promising of these can then be sent abroad for formal training. The essence of success in this part of the exercise is to keep valuations up to date by requiring regular statutory revaluations, say every five years. After the first valuation local officers should be available. Moreover, outside big cities, a much simplified form of valuation can be used in respect of all 'hereditaments'[2] except such things as department stores, large blocks of flats or offices and hotels. This will greatly reduce the cost. An adequate valuation is inevitably costly. This must be set against the low costs of assessment once the valuation has been made. It suggests, however, that a national government will be wise to organise the whole operation and pay for it out of national funds. In the U.K., after a long history of failure to get adequate valuation carried out locally, responsibility for it was transferred to the Inland Revenue in 1948.

The most satisfactory method of assessment is a flat rate pro-portional to the value of the hereditament. Urban authorities in development countries sometimes feel frustrated because they can derive so little revenue from the existing valuation, (which is almost certainly extremely out of date). They consequently plead to be allowed to use a progressive rate (or so-called sliding scale). It is a mistake for a national government to allow this, on two grounds. In the first place the proper place for progression in the tax structure is in the national taxes on income and wealth. It is important that this aspect of redistributional policy should be integrated with other aspects and not left to local option. Secondly (and this mainly concerns business hereditaments) there is no close correlation between size and profitability. Some industrial or agricultural types of production require much space in relation to the value of output, others require very little. In practice the attempt to apply a progressive scale to assessments leads to much artificial splitting up of properties in order to escape the high rate brackets, and so is inefficient and self defeating.[3]

1. Thus in Lagos it was found necessary to enlist the services of the 'White Cap' (leading) chiefs to determine boundaries in a slum clearance scheme; cf. my *Development from Below*, Oxford, 1961.
2. The technical term 'hereditament' includes the building and the plot of land on which it stands.
3. This has occurred in Jamaica where sugar estates are a very 'extensive' form of property.

One serious difficulty in collecting taxes of this type is the extreme sensitiveness of taxpayers, who find themselves in direct contact with the authorities in a way that is quite different from other taxes on outgoings, of which they are largely unconscious. This difficulty is present in an advanced country such as the U.K. as well as in a development country. It is consequently desirable to take very special steps to ensure that the purpose of the levy is understood, and to reassure taxpayers that it will be spent on something for which they have a real desire (such as education for instance). In the U.K. the distribution between services is explained in detail on the reverse of the Demand Note. In a development country more direct contacts, and purposeful public relations with taxpayers, may be necessary at least until the system is understood. In the U.K. in respect of small tenancies it is the custom to make the landlord responsible for collecting the rate with the rent. This system might be explored in a development country, but care would need to be taken to see that illiterate tenants were not overtaxed by unscrupulous landlords. This is of course by no means the only tax in respect of which such a danger exists.

Even when the hurdles of valuation and assessment have been safely crossed, there remain the troubles of collection. In the first place it is necessary to ensure that sufficient officers are available to institute a follow up of recalcitrant taxpayers; in the second that some sanction is available against persistent defaulters. In the U.K. there is a sanction of distraint in cases of refusal to pay after repeated warnings. The police have powers to enter the premises and to remove enough furniture to cover the rate charge. In a development country the taxpayer's possessions may not be sufficient to make this a feasible course. There are then two possible alternatives: either recourse must be had to the civil courts, or a threat of imprisonment made available. Clearly the latter is not desirable, although as a way of securing payment it is practicable in many development countries, where the social security system of the extended family is still strong enough to ensure that payment will be forthcoming. The difficulty of recourse to the courts is that the procedure tends to be very slow, so that tax arrears may get out of hand.[1] The possibility of a special court for rate cases should be examined.

---

1. This has occurred in Lagos. cf. Report on the Administration of Lagos Town Council by G. C. Jones and B. Keith Lucas, 1963.

From our discussions it will be evident that as revenue raisers taxes on outgoings have much to recommend them. Further, they can be of great use as controllers of mass consumption. But they are by no means perfect as a means of financing development. In the long run governments will find the need for an adequate system of taxing incomings, and they will be better employed in following up this line rather than dissipating their energies in experimenting with a wide range of (more or less substitutible) taxes on outgoings.

CHAPTER FIVE

TAXES ON INCOMINGS

1. *The Economic and Social Importance of Income Taxes*

THE earliest form of the taxation of incomings (as I think it is legitimate to regard it) was the obligation to perform regular services for an authority: working on the landlord's crops, repairing roads for the community, or in the case of prominent citizens, producing soldiers for the army. An obligation to perform regular services, for instance on the roads, lingered in some development countries until quite recently. Indeed there is not a great deal of difference between this and 'compulsory' work on community development projects. Generally speaking the service was inefficient and some sort of direct contribution came to be preferred by both parties. The next step in the taxation of incomings was the obligation to pay over in kind some proportion of the crop; this was frequently used to finance regular government services. Tax payment in kind lasted for long periods in many countries. In Japan it endured until modern times. There are some economists who still advocate its use in development countries, so that it is a possibility which we should briefly examine.

In a predominantly subsistence economy, where money is scarce, there is an obvious convenience if produce rather than its value can be paid over. It is easier for the government to exchange or distribute the 'revenue' than it is for the peasant to discharge his liability in cash. Payment in kind (not necessarily in crops[1]) can also be a useful way of introducing the idea that all should contribute to such basic public services as law and order. At a more advanced stage, when the effect of price changes begins to haunt an economy, tax payment in kind is a reinsurance to the government. It continues to receive the same real revenue in a situation in

---

1. Sir Harry Johnston, the first Governor of Uganda, permitted a wide range of payments, partly because he was anxious to collect examples of the fauna and flora, but basically because he was anxious to accustom the people to the idea that they must make some contribution. Ultimately surpluses of 'tax hippos' became somewhat embarrassing: cf. R. Oliver, *Sir H. Johnston and the Scramble for Africa*, Chatto and Windus, 1957.

which if taxes had been paid in cash it would have received pro-gressively less. The obverse of this, however, is that the taxpayer has to part with a correspondingly larger part of his real income to discharge his tax liability. He begins to insist that payment must be in cash. In Japan payment in kind endured so long because it was made in rice, the major farm crop and also the staple food of the country. The farmers always had rice and the government could always use it. These conditions were quite exceptionally favourable for the continuance of the payment in kind system, but ultimately the opposition of the taxpayer in face of rising prices broke the system.[1] In fact this will always be likely to occur, apart from the effect of greater familiarity with the conveniences of money and a more abundant supply of currency in rural areas.

As we have already observed, taxation of incomings in develop-ment countries is much weaker than the taxation of outgoings. One explanation of this is naturally the poverty of the inhabitants and the large proportion of them engaged in agriculture. Agriculture is hard to tax, and even in most advanced countries farmers tend to be undertaxed. As development proceeds it should be possible to raise the percentage of revenue derived from the taxation of in-comings from the present 10 per cent (or less), if not to the more than 50 per cent of the advanced countries, at least to 25 or 30 per cent.[2] This would be a great improvement both on economic and on welfare grounds.[3] It is our special task in this chapter to discuss choice in the field of the taxation of incomings, in order to judge what can be done to improve the contribution which they make.

The essential difference between taxes on incomings and taxes on outgoings is that the former require individual assessment of the circumstances of the taxpayer: his net income (or profits), his wealth and perhaps to some extent his family responsibilities. By contrast, in the case of outlay taxes, liability depends wholly on the value of the taxed goods consumed. The peasant and the millionaire pay exactly the same tax on a packet of cigarettes. Any tenant of a particular house will pay the same amount in rates irrespective of his income. The difficulty of taxing incomings is partly due to the

1. cf. R. P. Dore, *Land Reform in Japan*, cit.
2. Exclusive of export taxes on foreign owned companies; see below.
3. See the principles of taxation for development in the last chapter.

necessity for this individual assessment. Yet it is just this individuality which constitutes the chief attraction of these taxes for development. Each taxpayers' circumstances determine his tax charge. With a progressive tax structure, as his income rises he will automatically pay at a higher rate on the increment. In turn this will raise his average liability. This characteristic also gives to income taxes their distributional attraction: they can be very finely adjusted to ability to pay. Governments should remember, however, that additional liability to income tax is more inescapable than a rise in the rate of an outlay tax, and the taxpayer's reaction to a sudden increase will be correspondingly more violent.

2. *Varieties of Income Tax*

We shall consider taxes on incomings under three heads: (a) elementary substitutes for income and profits taxes, for example professional taxes, export taxes, schedular income taxes; (b) income taxes proper; progressive personal income tax, graduated personal tax and business profits taxes (impersonal income tax); (c) complementary taxes on incomings, such as taxation of capital gains, stamp duties, progressive 'expenditure' tax, gift and wealth taxes, real property taxes.

Apart from export taxes, to which we shall return in a moment, the taxes in the first group are not of great importance. For the most part they are inferior substitutes for a true income tax, and are usually recognised as such. Taxes on professions or occupations are not very different from licences. As we have seen, the primary purpose of a licence is regulatory, and regulation is certainly necessary in respect of a number of occupations (although it can usually more easily be taken care of by professional organisations). In the absence of an effective income tax it is tempting to impose a special charge on particular ways of making a living which seem regularly to bring in more income than others. It is a small step from this to what is known as the schedular income tax, a form widely used in the continental European countries and in their former colonies.[1] This form of tax frankly taxes different sources of income at different rates; partly on distributional grounds (some sources of

---

1. These countries now usually have in addition a surtax on global income above a certain (rather high) point. It is typically not very effective.

income are chronically more lucrative or regular[1] than others);
partly on economic grounds (the government seeks to expand or
contract supplies of particular skills).

If such a tax is carefully assessed on actual income from each
source it may bring in a fairly substantial revenue: but the schedular tax has two serious defects. In the first place it is impossible to
put a stop to lobbying by different interests demanding to have
their schedule lowered. Secondly, and ultimately more important,
it is impossible to assess a schedular tax progressively on total
income because the different schedular assessments are never
brought together. It is consequently wiser for a country to in-
augurate an income tax by attempting to cover all sources of income in the same assessment, and at the same rates (apart from any
special rebates it may be desired to introduce on social grounds or
to allow for the special costs of carrying on particular trades). If
trained staff is in short supply the exemption limit can be set high
at first, so that the number of assessments will not be beyond the
capacity of the administration.

As we have just seen one purpose of income tax substitutes is
regulatory. A particular type of regulation which calls for brief
mention is that of companies engaged in the search for, and exploitation of, minerals such as oil, bauxite, tin and copper. There
is a genuine conflict of interest here in that the country in which
the minerals are situated expects compensation for the removal of
part of its substance, perhaps at little benefit to itself—for instance
if the company concerned is owned abroad and is not willing or
able to undertake any processing in the country of origin (so that
the value added is minimal). In addition it wishes to have an
adequate share of what may ultimately be very high profits. On the
other hand the company, particularly if it is an oil company, feels
that it deserves special compensation for the high costs of pros-
pecting, in which a heavy risk element is involved.

The taxation of mineral companies generally takes the form of a
combination of royalties (representing the loss of resources by
extraction) and profits tax on the operations of the company. If
precautions have been taken (as suggested in the last chapter) to

---

1. Under British income tax income from work is taxed fractionally lower
than income from property. Originally this was to compensate for the greater
security of property income; in modern times the differential has been extended
as an incentive measure. Tax is, however, in all cases assessed on global income,
not separately on particular sources.

see that a separate local company is registered and to secure a
guarantee of minimum operation(and if possible processing), it
should be possible to extract most of the revenue by means of a
straight, undiscriminating, profits tax, keeping the royalty element
to a minimum. Royalties cannot be dispensed with, but they have
to be negotiated at fixed periods, when circumstances may have
entirely changed (for instance in the world demand for the
product). Negotiation is always difficult and apt to lead to
bad blood.

3. Market and Export Taxes

We must now return to the large group of taxes which are levied
directly on produce. One of the oldest is imposed on goods and
persons as they enter a tax jurisdiction. Known as *octroi* because it
has been much used in French speaking countries it is still an
important source of local revenue in certain Indian states.[1] Octroi
is particularly costly to assess and open to abuse since tax is collected at isolated boundary posts over which control is impossible.
The greater part of the revenue is derived from locally grown foodstuffs as they are brought into the towns. This tax has consequently
everything to condemn it: it is regressive and arbitrary, and directly
hinders the movement of goods and persons, which, as we have
seen, is so much in need of encouragement in development
countries.

An alternative method of taxing local farmers through their
produce is the market cess or market tax. These are easier to control
and so probably more equitable, since assessment and collection
take place at well defined centres, and subject to fairly adequate
inspection. They are, however, open to at least three objections. In
the first place, in so far as they are assessed on local foodstuffs
(which is typically an important element), they are, like octroi,
quite unnecessarily regressive. Secondly they are directly disincentive of the growing of cash crops, and so tend to throw farmers
back on subsistence agriculture. Perhaps the worst feature of these
taxes, however, is that only one type of occupation is taxed. Farm
incomes may well be lower than other village incomes and it is
inequitable that they alone should pay.

Market cesses are, like octroi, normally a local concern. A

1. A similar tax is the terminal tax imposed on the movement of persons, also
common in India.

national export tax is their big brother and suffers from many of the same defects. In so far as the producers whose output is subject to the tax are small farmers it may be considered to be a type of income tax; several governments have sought to justify export taxes in this way.[1] But again it only affects one type of activity: the production of one or a narrow range of crops. In so far as export tax falls on company or plantation produce it operates as an additional profits tax, which again is only very partial. There may occasionally be particular sellers' market conditions (such as occurred during the Korean boom of 1951) when the effective incidence of an export tax is on the foreign importers. It can then be imposed temporarily at high rates without fear of international repercussions. Indeed it may even be economically desirable in the interests of stability to impose a special export levy of the producers of a 'boom' commodity, since the ordinary company tax being proportional, not progressive, will not succeed in taxing them more heavily as profits rise.[2]

The more normal situation, however, is one of extreme competition among exporting countries, and a general buyers' market for primary commodities. In such a situation a country runs two very grave dangers in imposing high export duties, and thus increasing the cost of its output in international markets. In the first place it risks stimulating other producing countries to expand their output. Since, as we have seen, the range of tropical crops is small and many of them can be grown in a wide variety of conditions, ease of substitution is considerable. In the longer run a more serious danger is the development of synthetic substitutes. With the rapid progress which is being made by the chemists of the advanced countries no commodity can be considered really safe from synthetic competition. In respect of a number of commodities the substitutes are not merely good, but perfect. Only low selling prices can ensure that the natural product will not be superseded, and this leaves little room for export taxes.

From the budgetary point of view also, export taxes have the great inconvenience of a widely fluctuating revenue. Countries such as Ceylon and Uganda which have relied heavily on them for current budgetary purposes have found that their budgetary position deteriorates unmanageably when the prices of their primary

---

1. For instance Uganda.

2. Thus in 1951 the Swedish government imposed a special export tax on timber, but reserved the revenue for the future development of the industry.

commodities fall. Until effective income and profit taxes can be built up to take the place of export duties it is wise only to transfer a part of the revenue to the current budget, paying the rest into a fund to be used for budgetary stabilisation, and when a safe reserve has been built up, for development. Keeping export tax revenue partly outside of the current budget also gives opportunity for adjusting the rates of tax on a sliding scale varying inversely with the movement of prices.

4. *Personal Income Tax*

Enough has been said to indicate that all these income tax substitutes are inferior to the real thing. We must now make a frontal attack on the income tax problem. We have already discussed certain prerequisites for an effective income tax: assessment of global income from all sources by well trained and paid specialised officers;[1] complete identification of taxpayers, collections by a sufficiently large and reliable field staff to ensure that there is an effective follow up. While the broad lines of personal income tax can be the same in a development country as in an advanced one, there are certain social and economic differences which complicate the task of assessment in development countries.

Traders operating on their own are everywhere the most difficult class to tax according to their deserts. Probably they are in all countries taxed less heavily than they should be. This problem is magnified in a development country since the standard of accounting is low, and accounts may be kept in a local language which requires interpretation. There is little that revenue officers can do except exert steady pressure and see that interpreters are available where necessary.[2] Secondly, in an advanced country the taxable

---

1. British law requires that recipients of property income, or of global income above a certain point, must file accurate returns at the end of the financial year, i.e. after the income has been received. The returns are then checked by tax inspectors, with the aid of supplementary information, from employers, or (in respect of bank deposits) from banks. This procedure amounts to a tough 100 per cent check. American law requires a return at the beginning of the financial year, of anticipated income for the year. This normally results in the same return as last year unless a drastic fall is expected. At the end of the year divergencies between anticipated and received income have to be compensated. These are subject to a sample check only. The British system is clearly more accurate, but it is a good deal more expensive to operate.

2. The Shoup Mission in Japan attempted to improve the standard of accounting by allowing a rebate when firms made their returns on a special 'blue form'. The details required, however, were so much more exacting than what had customarily been demanded that the form was scarcely used.

unit is either a single adult or (according to British practice) a married couple assessed as a unit. In development countries a wider family relationship is common; perhaps an 'extended family' or group of three generations, or, in India, the 'Hindu Undivided Family' where a large number of relatives have legal sharing rights, whatever their ages or personal incomes. In these circumstances the definition of the tax paying unit is difficult; but Indian experience shows that solutions can be found (relatives over a certain number being subject to full tax according to their shares). Revenue authorities can also take comfort in the assurance that these traditional arrangements, which are essentially a form of social security, are on the way out before the march of Westernisation.

Advanced countries have normally been more concerned about the low rate of expansion of their populations than about overpopulation; hence it is usual to grant substantial allowances for a wife and dependent children, without limit as to numbers. A country threatened with a population explosion should be more circumspect, limiting the rebates to about two children. Allowances are the less necessary in development countries since children become subsidiary producers at an early age, and so are an economic advantage rather than a liability.

Many development countries have followed the advanced countries in introducing a system of current withholding (PAYE); some of them even extend this to cover day to day workers, the employer attaching stamps to a card.[1] Although the system cannot work in a development country with the same precision as in an advanced one, where every employed person is under a definite contract of service, in every development country (I believe) where a system of current withholding has been introduced, there has been an immediate improvement in revenue collections.[2] Without some such arrangement tax tends to be confined to government servants. It is most important that this should not happen, both on general grounds of equity and because of increased temptation to corruption where public employees feel they have a tax grievance.

In advanced countries the exemption limit for income tax is typically set at a point which includes as taxpayers the lower ranges

1. For instance Eastern Nigeria.
2. The difference has been especially remarkable in the Eastern Caribbean, as island after island has gone over to P.A.Y.E.

of clerical workers and the top ranges of manual workers (what may be termed the lower middle class range). From this point progression proceeds more or less regularly, by incremental stages up to a final increment (say 80–85 per cent) of net income. Broadly speaking this pattern can quite appropriately be used in development countries also, provided that the exemption limit is geared to the income distribution within the country. To use the same exemption limit as an advanced country implies that it is set far too high for either equity or control. The appropriate exemption limit depends, however, on whether there is in existence a graduated personal tax which will include the ranges below income tax as well as those within it. This is a matter to which we must presently return.

In the lower ranges of income tax it will not be possible to use a steep progression with equity, due to difficulties of assessment and collection. In the upper ranges, however, great efforts should be made to tax adequately both the rising tycoons (who will soon make their appearance) and large property owners—to the extent (as has just been observed) that the administration can cover equitably. There is strong distributional as well as economic justification for taxing the rich heavily in countries where incomes are very unevenly distributed, as they tend to be in all development countries. On the other hand many governments make the mistake of setting the final increments at a height which is (and is known to be) quite beyond the enforcement powers of the revenue authorities. This not only carries with it the danger of disincentive effect, but breeds a contempt for the law. There is even more justification for high taxation of incomes from property (including dues received by traditional authorities) since these are in no way functional to the development process. In some cases it may be possible to make use of the British device of imposing a higher rate on property than on earned incomes. This is a matter to which we must return in discussion of taxes supplementary with income taxes.

5. Graduated Personal Tax

We must now turn to consider the graduated personal tax, considered as a simplified income tax appropriate as the sole direct levy on the lower incomes and (in the interests of equity) as a first contribution from the incomes of the middle and upper classes, who will normally pay the regular income tax in addition. The G.P.T. is basically an extension of the hut or poll tax very commonly imposed in the early stages of development by a colonial power. In the modern refined form (in which Uganda was a pioneer) it bears a strong resemblance to the local income tax imposed in the Scandinavian countries,[1] and is also particularly suitable as a local tax. In development countries the G.P.T. is primarily geared to agriculture, and hence to rural rather than urban conditions. It can, however, be successfully used in urban areas, although with considerably greater difficulties of assessment.

Basically, as practised in Uganda (and now extended to Kenya),[2] the taxable unit is the family rather than the individual. This is inevitable in respect of agricultural incomes, which in rural areas are by far the most important element. Income from other sources —wages, salaries, trading, transport and so on—is then added in, giving a global assessment exactly parallel to normal personal income tax. No costs of making the income are allowed, and normally there are no dependents' allowances. This implies that it is essential to give the taxpayer ample means of appeal against an assessment which has become inappropriate because of a change of circumstances; but this is not difficult to work into the system.

The first stage in the assessment of the agricultural incomes element is to determine for each area (for instance a local government or court jurisdiction) a standard 'rate of return' per 'unit' on every source of income found in the area: so much per coffee tree in bearing (on the average, and with cultivation of reasonable diligence), so much per head of cattle or other farm animals, so much per fishing boat, per acre under a particular crop, and so on. These standard rates can be adjusted seasonally if necessary on account of climatic vagaries, but generally speaking they should hold for a short term of years, unless violent price changes are taking place. There must, however, be sufficient flexibility to allow for a crop failure in a particular year, so that income from that source can be drastically written down or omitted.

The next stage in assessment is for a small team of enumerators to visit each farm and record the number of units of each income source under the control of the tax family. To this must be added

1. See my *Development from Below*, and *New Sources of Local Revenue*, Report of a working party, Allen and Unwin, 1956.

2. On the strong recommendation of the Fiscal (Tress-Marshall) Commission Report of 1962.

details of income from non-farm sources. As with a conventional income tax, trading incomes are the most difficult to assess, but in this respect the local knowledge of the enumerators is a great assistance, since they are able to make use of indirect checks, such as estimates of stock in trade and turnover. Their greatest importance, however, is for the enumeration of farm animals, the numbers of which will be known to neighbours in a way that would be impossible for strangers.

When all sources of income have been ascertained they are entered, in triplicate, on a prescribed form, in the taxpayer's presence. He signifies his agreement either by signature or attested sign. This form virtually constitutes an income tax return. One copy is left with the taxpayer, and can be the basis of an appeal if he needs to make one. A second copy is preserved locally, while the third is forwarded to the appropriate higher authority, where it will be checked and the tax liability calculated, according to the rates ruling in the area. Experience shows that it is unsafe to leave the enumeration process to local landlords or traditional authorities (chiefs).[1] Where there is an established system of local government, the local secretary, one or two reliable councillors from the area, and one from a neighbouring district make a suitable body. The work is voluntary (as with the Swedish local income tax), so that costs are not heavy. If there is no suitable local body enumeration can be carried out by an official committee. This will be more expensive, and it is necessary to ensure that at least one of the members has sufficient local knowledge to check concealment of moveable sources of income. The process of checking returns and calculating the tax assessable is naturally vital. Although it is more automatic than enumeration, it is essential that it should be accurate, marred neither by errors of arithmetic nor by political bias. For these reasons it is better carried out by a higher authority.

There is no doubt that the G.P.T. works best where there is an established (although not necessarily sophisticated) system of local government to which a substantial proportion of the revenue can be allocated for the promotion of development in the area, along lines desired by the local community. (In all probability they will vote for more education.) Compliance depends very largely, however, on the method of payment adopted, and on the provisions available to deal with delinquency. The taxpayer will be informed

---

1. See allegations of the Cox Report in Sierra Leone, quote in *Development from Below*.

by the authorities as to the date and place where he should make his payment. Where there exists a major local crop it is obviously desirable to require the bulk of the payment to be made as soon as the crop has been harvested; but provision must also be made for payment by instalments, for it is unlikely that the tax family will have only one source of income. Each taxpayer will be given a receipt for what he has paid, and these can be checked by the local police, court messengers or similar semi-skilled officers. Since, however, the local taxing authority will also be working on a very narrow margin, and must have funds currently available (especially for wage payments), too much rope cannot be allowed to the tax-payer. As with urban rates (which we discussed in the last chapter) it may be necessary to introduce a fairly swift method of dealing with deliberate delay and delinquency, rather than wait for the slow process of the civil courts to take effect.

The best results from the G.P.T. are obtained where it is treated not as an isolated tax, but as the lower limb of a progressive personal income tax. Hence, although the revenues from the two taxes may accrue to different authorities, they need to be integrated into a system, without a gap, yet not getting in each other's way. National governments are often so nervous of the effect of any sort of local income tax somehow spoiling their own revenue that they refuse to permit the use of this important source of revenue, although they themselves would be unable to collect tax from the country people who form most of the G.P.T.'s assessees. This fear on the part of national governments is quite unjustified if proper steps are taken to organise the range and methods of assessment of the G.P.T. The Scandinavian example shows that this must be so.

Broadly there are two methods by which liability to income taxes may be assessed. The first and more primitive is the slab or range system: total income within a certain range is assessed to the same rate, in terms of a percentage, or more simply of a sum of money. This method is simple and easy to understand. For this reason it is often used for the G.P.T. although it has been abandoned in respect of most national income taxes. (It is still used, however, for death duties in the U.K., due to a fortuitous historical survival.) The slab system is, however, unsatisfactory for two reasons. First, at the point of liability to a higher rate the marginal rate of tax is extremely high, and this may well produce a disincentive effect to earning any more income. Secondly, if the amount due on each successive range is expressed in cash terms, the tax appears to be progressive, but in relation to the greater income it may in fact be proportional or even regressive, thus losing much of its distributional attraction. (This effect can be avoided if percentage rather than cash assessment is used but the marginal difficulty of moving from slab to slab remains.)

The alternative, and much more satisfactory, method of assessing income tax is the step or incremental system. Under this succeeding increments of income are assessed at progressively higher rates. Averaged over the successive increments the 'effective' progression takes the form of a smooth curve. The disincentive effect at the point of moving to a higher incremental rate persists to some extent, but due to the averaging of liability over the whole range of increments it is much weaker than under the slab system. It is desirable, both on grounds of distributional equity and of efficiency, to use the incremental system for G.P.T. in consonance with income tax, as soon as tax assessors and payers can be brought to an understanding of it. It will then be very much easier to integrate it with the higher ranges of income tax.

It was suggested above that it is advantageous to arrange for the bulk of the revenue from G.P.T. to accrue to local governments; we shall have to discuss this point more extensively in the next chapter. Here we should notice, however, that it will be necessary for the national government to impose some sort of ceiling on the local tax in order that its operation should not interfere with the national income tax. At the same time it is desirable that the local governments should be able to feel that it is *their* tax, by giving them some (limited) autonomy over rates and conditions. For instance they may be allowed to introduce a rebate to assist with school fees under certain conditions, or they can be allowed to operate a small degree of progression. By and large, however, it is desirable that the formula of G.P.T. should be proportional rather than progressive. This is desirable both on grounds of national distribution policy and because some local governments might be led to tax immoderately their few wealthy taxpayers. Even with a broadly proportional formula, however, G.P.T. will be a great improvement (both on grounds of equity and of revenue productivity) over a flat poll tax, the rate of which must inevitably be set very low so that the poor can contribute something.

The simplest ceiling which can be imposed on the G.P.T. is that of a maximum sum which local governments are authorised to extract from any taxpayer. This method is used in Uganda and

Kenya, where the ceiling is at present fixed at 600s. This method has, however, two disadvantages. If prices and incomes change substantially it will be necessary to raise the ceiling to prevent the local governments receiving less and less revenue in real terms. Further, at the point where the ceiling is reached the tax ceases to be proportional and becomes regressive, (since the 600s is an increasingly smaller proportion of income, as income rises). In order to avoid losing revenue on what may be a very important income range it will be necessary to arrange that the national income tax picks up the progression at this point. A more refined way of keeping the two taxes from overlapping is to lay down a maximum percentage that may be extracted by local governments. In Sweden this was fixed at 18 per cent. It is easy to arrange that the effective national tax rates should take off from this point.[1]

Before we leave the problems of taxing personal incomes it should be emphasized that G.P.T. is not merely a potentially important element in a comprehensive income tax system, but has very substantial merits in its own right. If it is mainly assigned to local authorities and some control over its structure is granted to them, G.P.T. can provide an excellent educational medium in respect of choice in the public services. It inculcates the realisation that local communities can by their own efforts acquire the public goods and services that they desire, but that at the same time they have to be paid for. Secondly, G.P.T. is a true global tax covering all sources of income and all taxpayers, as contrasted with market or produce taxes which hit only producers in particular lines. Finally, it will be noted, agricultural incomes are assessed on standard or potential income, not on actual income. Any output in excess of the standard is tax free. Hence the tax is incentive to improved effort (at least in some directions) rather than disincentive. Any community which has been accustomed to G.P.T. will have little difficulty in fitting into national income tax as their incomes rise.

6. *The Taxation of Business Profits*

Turning to the taxation of impersonal—profit—incomes we come to a very important element in the tax structure of development countries, in the future if not immediately. The League of

---

1. For further discussion of these problems see Report of the Fiscal Commission in Uganda, 1962, and *New Sources of Local Revenue*.

Nations did not recognise any prior right of countries where foreign firms operated such things as mines or plantations, to levy taxes on these installations. Indeed at that time very few of what are now the development countries levied any sort of profits taxes. Under the United Nations, however, the situation has been drastically altered. A clear prior tax right is recognised to the country where an undertaking is situated, relatively to that of the country where the parent company is registered and the majority of the shareholders reside. In order to encourage investment in development countries rebates on home profits taxes are also given by some countries, such as the U.S. Western Hemisphere concessions (which exempts from U.S. profits tax in certain circumstances), and the British Overseas Trading Corporation provisions of 1955. Generally speaking, so long as the development country has been careful to insist on the registration of a local company, and has taken powers to examine the company's books, there should be little trouble in taxing company profits. The form which the tax can best take, however, calls for brief comment.

Traditionally British income tax has embraced both personal and impersonal incomes, in so far as total company profits before allocation to dividends or reserves are taxable at a fixed 'standard' rate. So far as the shareholders are concerned, the whole of the amount thus 'deducted at the source' on their behalf from their dividends is credited to them against further tax liability. A substantial amount of personal income tax is thus collected without effort on the part either of the taxpayer or the revenue authorities, and with no possibility of evasion. So far as companies are concerned, up to the beginning of the Second World War, this taxation at the standard rate completed their liability. In 1946, however, an additional corporation profits tax was imposed, which now operates concurrently, and against which personal taxpayers receive no credit.[1] Countries with a British background have often adopted this traditional arrangement of taxing companies within the income tax, sometimes with and sometimes without the additional complications of a separate profits tax. It is very doubtfully worth their while to go in for such complications.[2] The chief reason for the inclusion of profits tax in income tax—the opportunity

---

1. The Labour Government (1964) has announced that it intends to go one step further and take company taxation entirely out of income tax, as is done in the U.S.A.

2. This was the view of the World Bank Team which reported on Uganda.

for deduction at source—is largely inappropriate where few of the shareholders reside in the taxing country. It would therefore seem more sensible for development countries to separate completely the taxation of personal and impersonal income, after the manner of the U.S.A.

The next problem is the height at which a profits tax may best be set in a development country. It should be made clear to start with that the place for progression is in the personal tax and not in the impersonal tax field. To tax companies at a higher rate merely because they are successful is to impose a direct brake on efficiency and enterprise; it is also unfair on their poorer shareholders. Development countries can rest assured that most companies prefer a straight, indiscriminating, profits tax, to the extent that they will be prepared to stand a fairly high rate (to which the parent company will already be accustomed in the country of origin) so long as they have some guarantees in other directions.

Manufacturing in a development country is subject to far greater risks than manufacturing in an already industrialised country. Neither the market nor the labour force will be ready made; they will have to be developed by the company's own efforts in the face of many unknown factors. Unforeseeable difficulties in respect of the acquisition of land are common; there is the danger of unexpected taxes, either at the local level (by tax on their land), or at the national level by an excise. There may also be a danger of nationalisation, or at the least of obstacles placed in the way of the transfer of dividends or capital. Many of these difficulties also beset locally owned companies, but they are more acute for the foreign firm because it is operating to some extent with remote control, and among peoples whose language and customs it probably understands very imperfectly. Hence any measures that the government can take to reduce the risks of investment will contribute directly to growth.

Risk reduction measures can be taken both outside and within the tax formula. They are likely to be more effective, however, if they form part of a unified policy. Non-tax risk reducers include the provision of accommodation on trading estates where land, communications and public utilities are already provided, assistance with the recruitment of the right sort of labour from technical schools, free import of equipment and so on. As pointed out earlier, matters are likely to go much more smoothly if the local Board of Directors includes members appointed by the government, or more appropriately by the Industrial Development Corporation, whose special care it should be to see that all avoidable risks are removed.

Within the tax system risks can be reduced and industrialisation encouraged along two paths, of which one sacrifices no revenue and should clearly be pushed as far as possible. The second route does sacrifice revenue, and so in view of the chronic need for funds in all development countries, should be indulged in with caution and moderation. Along the first route are indefinite carry forward of losses, quick[1] write off of the costs of capital equipment, and the concentration of depreciation allowances in the early years of the life of the asset (when the need for liquidity will be particularly great), by means of initial allowances or accelerated depreciation. Initial allowances can be varied both with the type of development which it is desired to encourage and also according to the volume of new investment which the economic and financial situation of the economy shows to be feasible. It does not contribute to true growth to encourage the starting of projects for which the means of completion will not be available.

Along the second route two types of measures are widely used: first the award of 'investment allowances', which are an extension of the idea of initial allowances, but make available a grant of more than 100 per cent of the cost of the equipment, and so constitute a definite present, not merely an advance payment, as in the case of the initial allowance. The investment allowance can be geared to the country's needs exactly in the same way as the initial allowance and applies to all firms, new or established. The second type of measure which sacrifices revenue but (if carefully used) does result in increased industrialisation is the tax holiday for new investment of a 'pioneering' nature. (The precise definition of a pioneer industry differs from country to country.)

A possible disadvantage of all these methods of stimulating industrialisation is that the benefit depends on the volume of fixed capital installed. It is sometimes feared consequently that they will swing the balance too violently in favour of capital intense methods, which may not be desirable in a country suffering from population pressure and a high level of unemployment. The pioneer/tax

---

1. It is advisable, however, not to permit a full write off in the year of acquisition, since this does in the short period sacrifice revenue, and also removes a potential instrument of control over investment. In Sweden instantaneous write off was permitted for a short period, but abandoned for these reasons.

holiday device is largely free of this defect and, moreover, it should
serve to give a direct stimulus to greater diversification in the
economy. Pioneer concessions, however, have the disadvantage that
they give no encouragement to expansion by established firms;
indeed they may even result in an increase in their tax burden.
The launching of new factories (or for that matter hotels) is never
costless to the government of a development country, even when
private enterprise provides the equipment and foreign exchange.
The government will be expected to provide communications and
public utilities, at the very least. In the case of hotels this is
particularly onerous since very high standards, for instance of
water, electricity and telephone supplies, will be necessary.

It would take us too far afield to discuss the various types of
incentive legislation with which development countries have
experimented, especially as there is now a large literature on the
subject.[1] It must always be remembered that so far as the assisted
firm is concerned, the benefit of a tax holiday is more psychological
than real in any effective fiscal sense. The usual tax holiday period
is five years (and it would sacrifice a great deal of revenue if it were
prolonged much more than this). Within that period it is not very
likely that a really pioneer firm will be making substantial taxable
profits, so that its gain is small. The highly successful firm has no
need of aid; the government sacrifices revenue to little purpose.
Real fiscal advantage can be written into the legislation, for instance
by starting initial allowances on the original equipment after the
holiday period is over, although it will then be five years old: but
the more such concessions are multiplied, the more revenue will be
sacrificed. A country which wishes to embark on incentive legislation in a big way should scrutinise very carefully each application, in order to satisfy itself that the proposed new enterprise is a
sound proposition which will really contribute to the growth of the
economy.

7. *Taxes on Capital Gains and Capital*

We must now turn to consider the third group of taxes on incomings: those that we have described as supplementary or com-
plimentary with income and profit taxes. These levies fall into two
groups: taxes on the transfer of capital assets and taxes on the value

1. Especially M. C. Taylor, *Industrial Tax Concession in Puerto Rico*, cit.

of the capital itself, unrelated to the income derived from it. In the first group taxes on capital gains are by far the most important. In practice the separate taxation of capital gains is not very widespread, but such taxes are strongly advocated in advanced countries for two purposes, first as a means of curbing speculation and secondly in order to stop up a favourite method of avoiding income tax by substituting capital for current receipts. The gains which are mainly caught by existing capital gains taxes are those which have been made on the stock exchange. Other gains, realised for instance from trading on organised markets and from speculation in land, are normally also subject to tax but they are more difficult to assess and are of minor revenue importance. Most development countries have only very limited stock exchanges, so that gains from this source are not likely to be important.

The problem of land speculation in development countries is, however, extremely important. Real estate is typically the most popular outlet for savings, because it is the best available hedge against inflation. Consequently land speculation very easily reaches unmanageable heights. It is essential to apply some curb to the propensity to buy land, since, apart from the push which rising land prices give to a generally inflationary situation, an uncontrolled land and building boom is inimical to sound development, diverting scarce resources from more fundamental constructional needs.

It is questionable, however, whether a capital gains tax is the best way of fighting land speculation, fundamentally because of the difficulty of identifying and valuing the units bought and sold. On the stock exchange every unit of a particular security is identical, so that there is no difficulty of valuation, at least so far as quoted securities are concerned. Even with unquoted securities the values are identical as between one unit and another. In respect of land this is far from being the case. There is no reason to suppose that a 'parcel' which is sold is ever identical with one which was previously bought, so that the assessment of the true capital gain on the realisation is virtually impossible. Fortunately there are other ways of fighting a land boom. Once a central bank has been established, interest and advances rates can be geared so as to reduce the loan funds available, and so diminish the attractions of speculation. Further, as we shall see presently, a tax on the capital value of real estate can be quite effective if the valuation process is carried out efficiently.

Other taxes on the transfer of assets which are commonly used are stamp duties and gift taxes. If stamp duties are levied on the seller (instead of, as is more usual, on the buyer), they operate as a minor capital gains tax. No development country can expect much revenue from this source, due to the small number of dutiable transactions. They are, however, a source of funds which should not be neglected in the general search for revenue. Gift taxes are advocated mainly in order to prevent the dispersal of fortunes which would otherwise be subject to estate or inheritance taxes. Gift taxes do not seem to bring in much revenue, no doubt because there are many loopholes whereby assets can effectively be used for the benefit of someone else without requiring a formal transfer. No country appears yet to have dealt successfully with this problem and we may conclude that a development country would be unlikely to do so.

The potential importance of inheritance taxes differs greatly from one development country to another. In tourist countries such as the West Indies there is undoubtedly some potential; but one of the attractions for wealthy people to retire to such places is just the absence of high estate duties to which they would be subject in their own country. It may well be better for a development country to encourage their residence, which will no doubt be accompanied by high spending, rather than to frighten them away by death duties. On the other hand estate taxes assessed on total assets at death are the most equitable and efficient type of capital tax, since a thorough valuation of the property can be made with no limit as to time.

We have to consider also, however, the potentiality of a tax assessed annually on capital (or wealth). Unless it is the intention gradually to confiscate property the rates of this must be set low enough for payments to be made out of current income. The effect is thus very similar to an income tax except for the fact that it does not impinge directly on effort, and so should be less disincentive of enterprise. It should be noted that a wealth tax is essentially a personal and not an impersonal tax; it should not be extended to companies.[1] There is no really satisfactory way of valuing the 'wealth' of a company. The nominal value of its shares is entirely irrelevant; moreover, the value of the assets depends not on their

---

1. This mistake was made initially in India, and companies found themselves without warning liable to 100 per cent increase in taxation. The company part of the tax was, however, soon discontinued.

individual (break up) worth but on their contribution as part of a going concern, and this cannot be isolated. Finally, to tax away capital which is being productively employed is to reduce the nation's capacity to produce.

The basic difficulty of an annual capital tax, even when it is confined to persons, is effective valuation, if an attempt is made to include a wide range of assets. Consequently it is not surprising to find that in those countries which regularly attempt to tax capital annually (the Scandinavian countries and the U.S. at the state level) the coverage is far from complete. Revaluations are carried out irregularly and partially. Indeed in practice it would appear[1] that so-called wealth or property taxes are little wider in scope than taxes on real estate. Even in the most advanced countries stock exchange securities figure to a very minor extent. There is little doubt that the equity of the wealth (or property) tax would be improved if its scope were confined to real estate. In fact this has been realised in many of the U.S. states. Consequently we may as well discuss it in this form. In fact we have approached very near to this in the last chapter, in our discussion of the tax (or rate) on the occupancy of land and buildings in urban areas.

Landed property is typically one of the earliest subjects of taxation. This is only natural, seeing that the greater part of wealth was commonly held in this form in early societies. Historically the greatest experiment in taxing land was the Land Revenue introduced into India by British administrators in the early nineteenth century, and still collected in spite of very great erosion of the revenue. It is worth pausing for a moment to look at this experiment, since the view still lingers that the importance of Land Revenue could be restored by relatively simple means. Under the influence of Ricardo and the Utilitarian[2] economists the Herculean task of valuing the innate potentiality of every plot of land in the sub-continent was attempted, the object being to tax away the surplus product of the better land over the product of 'marginal' land on which it was only just possible to make both ends meet. It was argued that the full effective incidence of the tax would be on the landlord, because an overcharged tenant would move away, and so

1. cf. Symposium on wealth taxes in different countries, in *Public Finance*, 1956.
2. For further detail see E. T. Stokes, *The English Utilitarians and India*, Oxford, 1959, summarised in *Development from Below*.

the tax would have no disincentive effects. This may well have been true in English conditions during the time of the Napoleonic wars and the Industrial Revolution, when Ricardo put forward this analysis. But the Indian peasant had neither the knowledge nor the opportunity to get away from an extortionate landlord.

In the event the task of valuation proved too much for busy administrators and the wiser of them confined the tax to what they believed was reasonable. Even so the peasants were cruelly burdened in many areas, and the shadow of this history still haunts attempts by Indian governments to extract more than a negligible revenue from rural areas, although the peasants are often no poorer than Africans who are paying quite high rates of G.P.T. Over the decades tax liability, fixed in money terms on wildly out of date valuations, has (as has been said) sunk almost to nothing. Adequately to restore the importance of land revenue would require a complete revaluation of rural areas, since drastically to increase rates at the old relative values would create intolerable anomalies. For the most part recourse seems to be taken in India and Pakistan to taxing produce rather than land; but this, as we have seen, runs into disincentive dangers, and is consequently less satisfactory than G.P.T.

The most promising future for the taxation of land in development countries lies, however, in urban areas. In the last chapter it was hinted that a tax based on ownership (or capital value) was superior for urban development to a tax based on rental (annual or occupancy) value. The reason for this is that the annual value of a plot depends only on the rent derived from it, including any building that has been erected on it. The capital or selling value of the same plot will, however, also include the market's valuation of the future use to which it might be put. In a rapidly growing urban area this will greatly exceed the capitalised value of the present rent. Consequently, if the capital base is used, as development takes place the base will automatically be strengthened and the government will collect a substantial share of rising land values. This will not only bring in a welcome addition to resources, but will (as suggested above) also contribute to keeping a land boom under control, since only a part of the increase in values will accrue to the speculators or developers. If from the beginning a record of title and register of sales prices is kept there will be no more difficulty —there may well be less—in carrying out valuations and revaluations on a capital than on an annual basis. The capital basis should consequently be used wherever possible in development countries.[1]

There remains one form of tax on incomings which it would be wrong to neglect completely, although what small experience of its operation there has been is not encouraging.[2] Paradoxically this is called by its author[3] an Expenditure Tax. The intention, however, is exactly parallel to an income tax, to impose a global and progressive levy on ability to pay; but ability is held to be more accurately measured by what is spent than by what is received. (It would take us too far afield to discuss this doubtful contention.) The primary purpose of the expenditure tax is, however, not so much to collect revenue as to encourage saving by the wealthy (to whom alone it would apply). Clearly savings which are never spent will be tax free and so should be encouraged; but those which are subsequently spent will have to bear a rate of progression which may well be higher than would have been the case under an income tax, so that their encouragement is by no means certain.

If a simple tax measure could really increase the propensity to save in development countries it would be an immense boon; but in practice the expenditure tax is not at all simple, because of the difficulty of discovering, and so assessing, personal expenditure in all lines. It is hoped by the author that a way round might be found by constituting the expenditure tax one of a group of interlocking taxes, the others being wealth tax, capital gains tax and gift tax. By assessing all these together it is intended to sew up the taxpayer completely so that all his transactions are revealed either by himself or by the other party to a bargain. As we have seen, the administration of these other taxes in development countries is normally not such as to inspire great confidence in the success of this device. But quite apart from this, the records which the taxpayer would be required to keep in order to make his return would be entirely beyond his powers. In fact this was the main reason for the repeal of the tax in Ceylon.

1. It would take us too far afield to discuss difficulties which may in fact arise in particular circumstances, from such factors as the existence of public domain (so that there are no true land sales) or even from imperfect and sluggish markets. Most of these are transitional troubles round which ways can be found. For further discussion see J. R. Hicks, 'Unimproved Value Rating', in *Essays in World Economics*, Oxford, 1959, pp. 237–44, and *Development from Below*.

2. It was in force in India for several years, but it is doubtful whether any revenue net of costs of collection was realised. In 1964 after an interval it was reimposed. In Ceylon it was withdrawn on grounds of impracticability almost at the start.

3. cf. N. Kaldor, *Indian Tax Reform*.

It seems inevitable to conclude that to bring about the increase in saving which is so urgently needed for development, reliance must be placed on the methods which we examined in Chapter 3, together with government savings achieved through taxation. Our investigations have shown that a very wide range of taxes are in principle applicable to development countries. We have noticed a number of reasons why in practice collections tend to fall far short of what is due. This is especially true of personal income tax. In this field personal and political relations sometimes make it particularly difficult to tax the wealthy adequately; but there is little doubt that the main obstacle to improvement is the insufficiency of the tax administration, both in terms of numbers and quality. There are a number of steps that development countries can take to improve this situation.

The problem needs to be tackled at two levels: (i) the lower level of the relatively large numbers of assessors and collectors; and (ii) the top level of much fewer real organisers of the service. Pakistan has set a useful example by establishing a Finance Academy which caters mainly for the first class. Special courses are given in tax techniques and also in economics (essential for officers who will be concerned with the assessment of business profits). In respect of the higher personnel it is probably advisable to send officers abroad for short courses and secondments so that they can observe for themselves the working of efficient tax offices.[1] When an income tax department is being established it is useful to borrow for a few years the services of an experienced tax officer from a country where income tax is well established. Even one such officer can make a spectacular difference to collections in the course of a very few years. There is no doubt that the additional revenue needed to finance development is largely lying dormant, and if it could be fully collected, it would go far to closing the gap, even at existing tax rates.

1. These are regularly organised for instance in the U.K. by the Royal Institute of Public Administration and the British Council in conjunction with the Department of Technical Co-operation. Secondments are arranged with the Inland Revenue, the Department of Customs and Excise, and if desired with local authorities.

CHAPTER SIX

INTERGOVERNMENTAL FISCAL AND FINANCIAL RELATIONS

1. *Planning and Federation*

IN any country where there is some decentralisation of decision making in the public sector problems of intergovernmental fiscal and financial relations necessarily arise. In this chapter consequently we shall be dealing with a very widespread if not universal phenomenon; but these relations can take as many different forms as there are types of political organisation. They will differ in scope and complexity both according to the constitutional provisions and to the traditions which the country has inherited from the past. Thus even when an entirely new constitution is being drawn up the constitution makers will not be able to make their sketch on a clean sheet; they will be hedged about by a variety of constraints which cannot be disregarded. Apart from the constraints due to tradition, there will be economic and administrative limitations, which, if they do not rigidly determine the allocation of certain taxes and responsibility for the execution of certain lines of expenditure to different levels of government, at least provide strong arguments in favour of particular arrangements.

The problems of intergovernmental financial relations are seemingly at their simplest in a unitary country; yet where there is a strong tradition of budgetary freedom and decentralised decision making, as there is in the U.K., matters may be complicated by the existence of several levels or tiers of local authorities, each with a range of powers and duties within its limited jurisdiction. Such are the 'county districts' (municipal, urban, rural, also parish councils) within the jurisdiction of counties, existing alongside the all purpose county boroughs independent of the counties within which they are situated. A complicated system of revenue sharing and grants has grown up to ensure that sufficient funds are available for all layers of government to fulfil their obligations while preventing a free for all competitive exploitation of limited local revenue sources.[1]

In an 'ideal' federation on the other hand there should be, according to Dr. Wheare,[2] no federal/state fiscal problems since both the 'general' and the 'state' governments should be politically and financially independent within their own spheres. (Since, however, local government is normally a state responsibility in a federation, the problems of the unitary country would still be encountered at that level. but probably on a reduced scale.) In practice, however, the ideal federation in this sense no longer exists (if it ever did in any complete sense), so that the problems of intergovernmental fiscal and financial relations turn out to be even more complicated in a federal or quasi federal country than in a unitary one. Consequently a major part of our discussion in this chapter will be concerned more directly with the federal rather than the unitary problem, although many of the problems are common to both. The fundamental differences between a federal and a unitary form of government is that in a federation the constituent units enjoy entrenched rights, embodied in a fairly rigid constitution, while in a unitary country the local units are statutory bodies whose powers and duties are derived from the central government, and so can be altered by it at any time by simple legislative process. In a federation each state has its individual constitution which is only alterable by its own decision. This implies incidentally that it controls the position of its own local authorities, so that the general government can only exercise any influence over them through the states by persuasion.

In considering intergovernmental fiscal and financial problems it is useful to classify them under four heads, two on current and two (mainly)[3] on capital account. Of those on current account

1. In the U.K. this is achieved by making the county districts the sole taxing (rating) authorities outside the county boroughs. In the counties the upper layer (county councils) and the lower layer (parish councils) 'precept', i.e. require the districts to raise revenue for their needs. The county precept invariably greatly exceeds the requirements of the actual rating authority, owing to the fact that education is a county responsibility. This system of layers of local government with precepting was tried out in West Africa during the 1950's, but it proved impossible to get it understood, so that it had to be abandoned; cf. *Development from Below.*

2. cf. K. C. Wheare, *Federal Government*, Oxford, 1963.

3. Some items which in the national accounting sense would be on capital account are in practice dealt with by current means.

the first is concerned with rights to levy certain taxes by federal and state governments respectively. Secondly come rights to enjoy certain revenues, either derived directly from taxes or by transfer from another level of government (almost exclusively from a higher to a lower level).[1] We shall find that this distinction between the allocation of rights to levy (and so determine the rates and conditions of a tax) and of rights over the produce of a tax is fundamental in problems of federal finance. These rights will naturally be entrenched in the constitution in some manner. It will simplify future relations, however, if they are not spelled out in too much detail, especially so far as the exclusive rights of the federal government are concerned. Experience shows that too great a rigidity of allocation may seriously impede the making of adjustments, because of such things as a change in economic circumstances—or changes in the conception of taxes—even although all are agreed that the adjustments should be made.[2]

Intergovernmental relations on capital account are concerned first with the right of different layers of government to raise loans, secondly with rights and duties in respect of planning and economic development. Problems concerning both these relations also arise in a unitary country but they are much less awkward, largely because they are more subject to central control and also because the units are usually smaller than in a federation. In the older federations uncontrolled borrowing by the states gave rise to repeated trouble and led to the virtual bankruptcy of certain states. This was especially true in Australia. As a result of this experience most of the older federations have now evolved orderly devices and practical methods of co=ordination. The newer federations should be able to benefit by this experience, choosing those arrangements which seem most suitable for their circumstances. These we shall discuss below.

But planning for economic development, and particularly the construction and finance of fixed capital formation, presents problems in federal finance that are essentially new. India has been

1. This follows from the chronically weaker fiscal position of lower layer authorities (see below, p. 124). In several African countries, it is true, local authorities have from time to time been required to share the tax with the central (territorial) government; but this arrangement was normally regarded as, and always proved, temporary.

2. The most famous historica case of this was the prolonged difficulty in the U.S.A. over introducing a federal income tax, because of the constitutional provision that personal taxes must fall equally per capita throughout the Union.

a pioneer in federal and state planning since 1950. Other development countries have all enthusiastically followed suit. It cannot be said, however, that those which are federations have any of them yet found a very satisfactory method of co-ordinating national and state plans and their finance. In this field the older federations have much less experience to offer than in respect of borrowing policy and debt service, since they were already largely developed by the time that planning became feasible. (Of the older federations the recent experience of Australia is probably the most helpful.)

Intergovernmental problems of capital development and its finance are made especially difficult by the fact that they are very closely related to what are now regarded as fundamental responsibilities of national governments: the promotion of economic development at the fastest rate consistent with reasonable economic stability and full resource usage. These responsibilities did not enter into consideration when the older federations were finding their feet; but in the newer countries where 'nation building' is a high priority, they have become vital. In the present chapter we shall confine ourselves to the fiscal aspects of these capital account problems, leaving broader issues for later consideration.

A federal constitution is normally more costly than a unitary one covering the same area, due to the multiplication of legislatures and other overheads. In principle it is not impossible that a union of previously independent units might be so much more efficient that there would actually be economies in administration for the whole area.[1] Even so a single unitary constitution would almost certainly be cheaper to run. In view of this costliness of federalism there must clearly exist reasons why less than unitary constitutions are chosen. These reasons may be either social, including racial and religious differences, or they have a politico-economic basis: the two sorts of influences are not always clearly separable, but a difference in weighting can usually be discerned. The choice of a non-unitary constitution is evidence that the citizens of one area are not prepared to treat their co-citizens in

---

1. This would almost certainly be the case among the little islands of the Eastern Caribbean, some of which suffer severely from diseconomies of small scale. Federation could lead both to economies at the legislative level and to a lowering of administrative costs through greater efficiency and a wider choice of personnel.

another area entirely all fours with themselves, although at the same time they are willing to pool such fundamental public responsibilities as defence and external relations. The consciousness of these differences, which require the maintenance of a wide range of individuality among the units, may vary enormously in intensity and so give rise to a great variety of constitutional relationships. These will be directly reflected in the fiscal arrangements on which it proves possible to reach agreement among the units.

2. Types of Federal Association

Broadly speaking there are two opposite origins of federal relationship: (i) where a previously unitary state breaks up owing to the inability of the constituent units to continue in such close relationship (this has been called federation by disaggregation); (ii) where a number of previously independent units agree to come together for certain purposes but are passionately desirous of maintaining their own individualities, as they could not in a unitary state (federation by aggregation). The attainment of independence appears to show up differences which were previously submerged and thus gives rise to federation by disaggregation. This has occurred both in India and Nigeria; but it is always likely to be a rare phenomenon, since it is one thing to give up the advantages of a unitary state and quite another to wish to assume them without previous experience. On the other hand there are many reasons which may draw previously independent units together, such as the desire for greater economic or political power, the hope of saving some of the costs of separate existence, or merely the wish to combine certain services of common interest.

The simplest form of common relationship is the Customs Union or Common Market. It is tempting to regard this as a first step towards closer standing together; but experience shows that the further steps may be very much delayed. The union may be entered into without any clear acceptance of a political federation, as has been apparent in two contemporary Common Markets: Western Europe and the three Commonwealth East African countries. Both of these have developed common institutions and services which go considerably further than a bare common tariff, and have stood firm for a number of years without any specific action having been taken towards closer union. On the other hand it is clearly possible to conceive of political federation without a customs union. This was indeed the position in the Federation of the West Indies, and certainly the failure to attain agreement on a common tariff was not the sole or perhaps even the most important reason for the breakdown of the federation.[1] On the whole it seems probable that neither a bare customs union nor a federation without a common tariff can be regarded as stable institutions.

At the other extreme are federations where the central government is so powerful that the working of fiscal and financial relations approximates in some, perhaps many, ways to that of a unitary country. In this way formerly South Africa exhibited a number of federal attributes. In India, as might be expected of a federation by disaggregation, the Union government is extremely strong vis à vis the states, and the impact of planning has made this even more pronounced. Yet it would be a complete misconception to claim that India is a unitary state. On the other hand the Nigerian federation by disaggregation appears to be developing into a rather exceptionally loose federation, whatever may have been the intentions of its founders.

From this discussion we may draw two conclusions. In the first place almost any degree of political or economic tightness or looseness may exist, and each federation will consequently have to solve in its own way the problems of federal finance. Secondly, no federation ever stands still; there is a continual process of shift in the relative posers of the centre and the units. Usually the shifts work in the direction of strengthening the centre vis à vis the units. This is probably inevitable in view of the strength of the desire for a national policy; but the shift in emphasis may be neither large nor rapid, nor need it be continuously in the one direction. There may well be a see-saw movement around a trend which is broadly in the direction of closer national unity—unless indeed the whole association dissolves. In any association it may be many years, even decades, before constitutional amendment catches up with a *de facto* shift of emphasis.

When the union becomes close enough for the general government to qualify not merely as a federal but as a national arbiter of

---

1. At the time of the withdrawal of Jamaica, which led ultimately to the break up of the federation, a customs agreement was nearer than is generally realised; cf. Report of the Trade and Tariffs Commission, Government of the West Indies, 1958.

policy, there are certain additional powers and responsibilities which must of necessity accrue to it, over and above its fundamental duties of defence and relations with other independent countries. Fiscal allocation needs to be adjusted accordingly. The most important of these additional national requirements are three. First comes responsibility for the whole gamut of international economic as well as political relations, including the good health of the balance of payments. (In some ways this responsibility may be regarded as an extension of the fundamental duties of a federal government, but in practice much more is required because of the economic and statistical problems involved.) Secondly, the national government acquires a pre-eminent responsibility for stable development. This implies that it must have the means for national plan making and implementation with the fiscal rights and controls necessary for the purpose. This inevitably implies a substantial curtailment of state rights. Thirdly, it will generally be agreed that the national government should exercise a general responsibility for policy in respect of the distribution and redistribution of incomes throughout the country. This responsibility has a personal aspect reflecting an ideological conviction that differences between rich and poor citizens should be reduced. (We have seen that they tend to be much wider in development countries than in advanced countries.) Income redistribution has also an inter-local aspect leading to a desire for special help or privileges for the poorer and more backward areas.

The consciousness of the importance of such problems and the demand for the national government to follow an active policy in respect of them differs substantially from one country to another. This is very noticeable among unitary countries; by no means all of them hold with the policies of a welfare state and all that it implies in respect of income redistribution. Among countries with federal forms of government differences are, not unnaturally, still wider, for, as we have seen, the choice of a non-unitary constitution largely turns on an unwillingness to put related people's interests on the same footing as one's own. In a federation particularly, but also to some extent in a unitary country, there may be a lurking suspicion that an over active policy of income redistribution (especially inter-local redistribution) will be contrary to the national interest, in that it removes from the more promising areas resources which they could use more productively than the poorer areas. For a development country this constitutes a very difficult dilemma, since the need for growth is vital, but the poverty of the backward areas may well be shattering. The conflict of interests which results has both a national and a local aspect. These impinge most directly on arrangements made for revenue allocation on current account, but are also intimately connected with the siting of capital works.

3. *Tax Allocation between Federal, State and Local Governments*

We must now consider what broad fiscal arrangements will be appropriate to these extended responsibilities of national governments, bearing in mind the continuing responsibilities of the unit governments also. In the first place responsibility for international economic relations, and particularly for the health of the balance of payments, implies national control of the rates and conditions of those taxes which impinge directly on the balance. Chief among these are import duties. Once a federation has been established agreement on this appears to follow quite naturally. Experience shows, however, that this is the first and perhaps the most formidable hurdle to be crossed in setting up a federation by aggregation. (In a federation by disaggregation the common tariff will normally be taken for granted.) The difficulty of establishing a common tariff is that before federation the smaller and poorer units will probably have been relying on import duties as their main source of revenues. To give them up has a shattering effect on their budgets, which they have not the alternative means to avert. A way can usually be found round this difficulty by the stronger units agreeing to accord the weak ones special concessions, which are hoped to be temporary. (Like all such things, however, they have tended to endure long after their expected demise.) Thus Western Australia and Tasmania received special help, as did (and does) Prince Edward Island in Canada. In the West Indies the situation was complicated by a new factor, which in modern conditions might occur at any time. Before federation the two high tariff islands were Jamaica and Grenada. The latter is relatively poor, although by no means the poorest. Compensation for loss of revenue would have been quite feasible. Jamaica is, however, by a considerable amount the richest of all the islands save Trinidad (with her oil), and compensation would clearly have been inappropriate. Yet a substantial amount of control over her imports was a necessity for Jamaica since she had before federation embarked on a process of accelerated development, and was sailing as near the balance of payments wind as she dared. Her revenue needs were also so urgent that a right to impose import quotas would hardly have been sufficient to meet her needs.

As an interim solution it was suggested (in the event unsuccessfully) that each unit should be free to levy at rates chosen by itself, what were called 'consumption duties'[1] on a limited range of products (beer, spirits, tobacco and petroleum products), provided there was no discrimination of rates according to country of origin—whether local, from another unit in the federation, or from abroad. This was effectively a sales tax on a limited range of goods. Seeing that the need for revenue was so pressing it would have been unlikely that unit would have charged such high rates as to kill consumption. The effect would not have been likely to influence the balance of payments seriously. This idea is probably capable of application to other federating areas which may find difficulties in coming to agreement on a common tariff.

The two other taxes which impinge on the balance of payments are excise and export duties. They are obviously much less important than import duties, but nevertheless deserve some consideration, especially as the question of control is likely to arouse more controversy than will occur with import duties, once the common market is accepted.

Excise duties are frequently imposed on the home production of commodities which would bear an import duty if produced abroad. This would seem to constitute an argument for assigning them to the national government. Yet they impinge only indirectly on the balance of payments, so that there is no compelling economic need to do so. At the same time it would be a mistake to allow the states a free hand over them. As we have seen, nothing is more likely to choke off entrepreneurs than the fear of additional taxes just when their infant industry is beginning to find its feet; this again suggests national control. On the other hand it must be borne in mind that excise duties were one of the twin pillars of state (then provincial) finances in India for many decades prior to independence (the other being land revenue). Almost the whole of the revenue was derived from liquor and tobacco, and it was only the impact of prohibition which put an end to this arrangement, driving the states into the more devious paths of sales taxes

1. Report of Trade and Tariffs Commission, cit.

(which we shall examine below). It would seem consequently that a strictly limited range of excise duties could safely be assigned to states, as a source of independent revenue in case of need.

Export duties are more complicated; it cannot be denied that they impinge directly on the balance of payments in so far as they reduce the volume of exports. On the other hand, in view of the danger of substitutes, export duties can only safely be imposed at very moderate rates. There is the further consideration that products which can be made subject to export duties are frequently located only in certain areas.[1] This would perhaps constitute an argument for state control. On the other hand the fluctuating revenue to which export taxes are subject makes them more manageable in the national than in state budgets. Finally, the argument has been advanced that as a species of income tax export duties should be controlled by the same level of government which controls the personal income tax. This would normally be the national government. But as we have seen, export taxes are a good way off being a true income tax, so that the argument is somewhat weak. Again it would appear that there are no compelling arguments on either side, so that the criterion of independent state revenue needs can once again be used. We shall return to this question shortly.

In discussing the allocation of export taxes we have already entered the field of taxes on incomings. One of the most controversial issues in federal finance is the control of income taxes, personal and impersonal. Its responsibility for economic stabilisation implies that a national government needs to have control over the level of disposable incomes and profits. Responsibility for income distribution (in so far as this is considered important) implies in particular that the national government should be in control of the progressive element of tax on the larger incomes. Moreover, revenue derived from this level is likely to be more fluctuating than revenue from the whole body of income tax payers. This constitutes an additional argument in favour of central control.

But the main argument for national (rather than unit or concurrent) control of income tax is that states will inevitably impose

---

1. The most striking instance of this phenomenon is Nigeria, where the different export product areas closely follow regional boundaries. The taxes are administered by the federal government, but the whole revenue is returned to the region of origin.

different rates and progression if left to themselves. Poor states will tend to make rates high and progression steep, so far as they can do so without unduly stimulating emigration; so also will states with a strong redistributional ideology. In an emergency the national government will want to take over state income taxes so as to raise the rates. (This happened in both Canada and Australia during the Second World War.) The national government will not be able to charge much more in the high tax states, so that the whole burden will fall on the others. As a result of this experience in neither federation have the units recovered their former control, and it would appear that the states are now reconciled to federal control as a permanency.

In a development country it may be argued that these reasons for national control of personal income tax are not operative. The opportunities for compensatory finance are negligible and the claims of income redistribution are not strongly felt. This argument led the Raisman Commission, when setting up the tax system in Nigeria,[1] to transfer the whole of personal income tax outside the federal territory to the states (regions); with the provision that in the event of a defence emergency the federal government might take over control, but strictly only for the duration of the emergency. In view of the widely different levels of regional income tax which are already operating it is doubtful if this provision could be effectively operated.

Initially in a development country income tax will probably be in its infancy, so that if should not be difficult to start with national control and all that it implies for efficiency of administration. In this way the troubles experienced in Canada and Australia (and perhaps yet to be experienced in Nigeria) can be completely forestalled. It should be noted, however, that all that has been claimed so far is that the progressive (surtax) element of income tax should be under national control. This need not interfere with state or local control of a low level proportional tax such as G.P.T. We must return in a few minutes to discuss the possibilities of various methods of income tax sharing.

The arguments for national control of the rates and conditions of impersonal (business profits) taxes are even stronger than those for the control of progressive personal taxation. It is usual for manufacturing and other business to operate on an interstate basis and it is highly inconvenient for firms to be faced with

1. Report of the Fiscal Commission 1958, Cmd. 481.

different taxes on branches situated in different areas. Closely related to this consideration is the wisdom of having a common company law operating over the whole country. Regulations concerning the starting, merging and winding up of companies have a fiscal as well as a legal aspect. This is even more apparent in relation to arrangements for loss carry forward and depreciation provisions on fixed capital. Above all it is desirable to bring incentive legislation, including provision for tax holidays and pioneer concessions, under unified management. Competitive bidding between units can only lead to a general loss of revenue.

Thus we find that there are strong arguments for national control of import duties, of most income and profit taxes, and probably also of export taxes, with excises remaining an open question. We must next ask whether there are any other generally used taxes for which a particular layer of government is clearly indicated. This question can best be approached by considering the requirements of state and local budgets. The basic necessity for these, but particularly for states in a federation, is that their governments should have sufficient independent revenue sources to permit them to carry out a full budgetary exercise without interference. By independent sources (in addition to any trading or investment income) is implied taxes of which the governments concerned can choose the rates and conditions, although naturally only within the broad framework set by national policy. Such autonomy is essential for a full budgetary exercise because this must include the possibility of varying the size and composition of the revenue side as well as of the expenditure side of the account.

In addition, as we have seen, it is desirable that taxes under the control of lower layer governments should not be subject to inherently fluctuating revenue. The smaller the jurisdiction of the government concerned the greater its need for steady incomings, to compensate for its restricted power of manoeuvre and the rigidity of its obligations. From the administrative point of view taxes assigned to lower layer governments should be easy to assess and collect. Even in a federation the general level of state administrations tends to be lower than those of national governments, and this is even more true at the local level. Finally, it is a great convenience if the base of taxes for lower layer governments can be unequivocally localised so that there is no dispute over jurisdiction.

So far as local governments are concerned there is one obvious answer to these conditions: a tax on land and buildings in the area. Our previous discussions have revealed that there are many varieties of this tax. So long as the expensive and difficult task of valuation is carried out regularly by a higher layer government, even small authorities should be able to manage the assessment and collection of this tax without difficulty. The fact that this tax—or family of taxes—takes the form of a rate or poundage on a fixed valuation makes them particularly suitable as a balancing factor in local budgets. When all other incomings have been determined and set against outgoings it is simple to calculate what 'rate' needs to be set in order to balance the budget. We may hence conclude that taxes of this type should be reserved for local governments. In a federation they would consequently be ascribed to the states, because local government is a state matter; but the states would almost certainly find that they had to hand them over to local control. There is one difficulty, however. We have seen that this tax, while eminently suitable for urban conditions, may be difficult—or even impossible—in rural conditions if there is not individual land ownership. For these conditions we can still have recourse to the G.P.T.; but this brings us to questions of income tax sharing for which we are not yet quite ready.

4. *Sales Tax as a State Levy*

We have now succeeded in finding taxes which should be under national control and a tax which is eminently suitable for local government. Even in a unitary country this one tax may not be sufficient for the needs of local independent revenue; we shall return to this point when we come to discuss transfers from higher level governments. So far as a federation is concerned, however, we have not succeeded in finding any tax which is inherently suitable for the states. As we have seen, excises are a possibility. Some or all of the taxes on motoring may also be transferred to them, but since cars and motorists are very mobile, there cannot be much variation of rates as between one state and another.

A third and more promising possibility is a low rate general sales tax assessed on a wide range of consumers' goods. It must be noticed that this tax provides on the average over 25 per cent of state revenue not only in the U.S.A. (which is easily under-standable) but also in India, where conditions of retailing are by no means more orderly or sophisticated than in other development countries. Because of its relevance to other development countries Indian experience of state sales taxes merits a brief discussion. Taxes of this nature are not generally regarded as 'good' taxes. As we have seen they tend to fall on goods that are in common, if not in basic, use. Their anti-welfare qualities are, however, con-siderably mitigated by the fact that their wide coverage enables a very substantial revenue to be raised at rates so low as to be tolerable even on small incomes.

In India the first state sales tax appeared in Madya Pradesh (then Central Provinces) in 1925. There is now no state that does not impose it; but the process of generalisation has been slow. The Union government made virtually no effort to regularise state' taxes before 1945;[1] by that time the states were well en-trenched. As we have seen, the collapse of excise revenue made the development of other tax sources imperative. The scope of sales taxes differed widely from state to state. Some were single point (retail), others covered production, wholesaling and re-tailing, and so tended to be badly pyramided. Some spread their net so wide that even local foodstuffs were included. Over the years some orderliness has been introduced, although this required con-stitutional amendment. The most recent limitations exclude trans-actions outside the state, imports and exports over the national boundary, interstate trade (subject to Presidential waiver), and all goods declared essential to life. Further, taxes on certain types of sales have been transferred to the Union list and have been amalgamated with Union excises, the states receiving compen-sation. The result has been an improvement in efficiency, but the greater part of the additional revenue seems to have accrued to the Union Government.[2]

It would be rash to claim that in all the states the administration of Indian sales taxes reaches a high or perhaps, on normal stand-ards, even a tolerable level. As one would expect it does very well in the richer states and is inefficient and unpopular in the poorer

---

1. For information concerning sales taxes in India I am indebted to an (as yet) unpublished thesis, 'Union State Finance in India', by Dr. N. A. Rao, Karnatik University, 1963.

2. See D. R. Singh, 'Substitution of Excise Duty for Sales Tax', *Economic Weekly*, 11 July 1964.

parts of the country. By and large, however, there is no doubt that it works, as the following quotation[1] reveals.

> Sales Tax owes its present position ... not merely to the size of its yield, but to the expansiveness which its inherent elasticity and wide coverage imparts to the fiscal structure of the state ... . By comparatively simple process of adjustment of the rates and incidence of the sales tax ... or by modification of the structure of the tax ... the state can, with singular efficiency, regulate its revenues within fairly wide limits.

The basic economic drawback to state sales taxes is the hindrance to interstate trade, not so much perhaps of physical difficulties, but because of the confusion to business of a multiplicity of tax formulae. On this account the national government might decide to restrict the autonomy of sales taxes fairly drastically, while still recognising their value. In compensation a state tax on value added might be considered. As we have seen the incidence of this is very similar in most circumstances, and it is relatively easy to administer. Since the number of firms included in the T.V.A. would probably be less than in a sales tax, it would be easier to handle and might also serve to stimulate state activities in promoting industry.

5. *Methods of Income Tax Sharing*

Most of the taxes which we have considered so far as suitable for state operation fall on outgoings. In Scandinavia, as we have seen, local authorities enjoy an income tax with a ceiling as high as 18 per cent of all incomes. In a federation it is difficult to deny the states some stake in personal income tax more considerable than the G.P.T. Sharing of personal income tax by different levels of government can be arranged in a number of ways. The simplest and crudest is simply to allow the lower levels concurrent rights. Thus in some parts of the U.S.A. taxpayers are simultaneously subject to federal, state and city income tax. If concurrent rights are granted some priority must be given to one of the levels in order to ensure that the aggregate does not exceed 100 per cent of income.

An improvement on this procedure is to allow states to add a percentage to the national levy for their own use. This 'centime

---

1. cf. Report of the Bombay Sales Tax Enquiry Committee, 1957–58.

additionel' or surtax method has several advantages. It secures
an integrated tax and it is administratively efficient, since assessment and collection will be the responsibility of the national
government. As with concurrent exploitation the states are free
to choose their own rates of tax (although a ceiling may be imposed), but as regards conditions and rebates they have broadly
to follow national policy. Serious differences between state levels
of tax can be prevented by a ceiling which will, at the same time,
ensure that no tax tops 100 per cent.

India illustrates a third method of income tax sharing. The
Union government has been given a constitutional obligation to
distribute a percentage of income tax revenue to the states. The
precise percentage was initially at the choice of the national
government, but it would be very difficult for it now to reduce the
state share. The advantage of this device is its administrative
simplicity. But, as will be apparent, it is strictly speaking a
method of *revenue* sharing, not of tax co-operation. The states
have no say in either rates or conditions. It also has the disadvantage that should the Union government wish to restrict
consumption via the income tax it can only do so at the cost of
making the states better off from the increased tax collections.
For this reason the Indian government now protects its position
by means of a corporation tax, the revenue from which is not
distributable. There remains the problem, common to all methods
of revenue sharing, of the distribution of available revenue between
the different states. To this we must return in a moment.

It should be clear however that of all these methods of income
tax sharing something along the lines used in Scandinavia, and
suggested above in relation to the G.P.T., is the most satisfactory.
It preserves to lower layer governments a substantial autonomy
in choice of rates and conditions; it in no way interferes with
overall progression, and so with national distribution policy.
Finally it protects lower layer governments from fluctuating revenues to a much greater extent than any of the other methods,
since the lower layer tax is only concerned with the relatively
steady section of income tax.

Although there are thus a number of sources from which state
governments can hope to derive revenue, it is only too likely
that in the aggregate they will not bring in a great deal, very
much less for instance than the federal government will be raising
from import duties. If, as is probable, the states have main

responsibility for education and public health as well as a predominant share in road works, there will inevitably be a serious
imbalance between the states and the federal government. The
national government will tend to have more than it needs, while
the states will not be able to perform their duties without a considerable amount of help. This imbalance is in fact typical of
almost all federations; it is naturally more serious for the poorer
states who have less opportunity of raising autonomous revenue,
and for this reason it tends to be a more serious problem in a
development federation than in an advanced one. The imbalance
will have to be corrected by transfer from the federal to state
budgets in some way; as we shall see there is a wide field of choice.
It must be borne in mind that there is a double problem to solve,
first that of determining the size of the transfer and secondly
of deciding its allocation between the different states. The two
problems are connected, because some methods of allocation will
enable the national government to carry out its policy (for instance of
inter-local redistribution of income) more economically than others.

6. *The Correction of Fiscal Imbalance*

The simplest method of transfer is to require the national
government to hand over a stated percentage of certain taxes
in accordance with the source (or derivation) of the revenue. This
by itself is not likely to give satisfactory results, for two reasons.
In the first place it may be virtually impossible to determine the
derivation of a number of taxes—for instance general import
duties—unless indeed each state has a separate port of entry
which is exclusively used. It is a good deal easier to distribute
excise tax revenue according to derivation because tobacco and
beer, the two main exciseable commodities, will be manufactured
in a few main centres. With the co-operation of the companies
concerned a very close approximation to true derivation can be
found. Secondly it is obvious that the wealthier a state the better
it will do in the derivation share out, so that the operation will be
anti-redistributional. This is not necessarily of first importance,
especially in the early stages of development. It may well be in
the best interests of the G.N.P. that the most go ahead states
should be helped to develop. They will probably make much
better use of the funds than the more backward states.[1] This is

1. cf. I. M. D. Little, *Aid for Africa*, Pergamon Press, 1964, where this
view is put very strongly.

a dilemma which we encountered earlier. It has to be settled by each country for itself.

In view of the anti-redistributional tendency of transfer by straight derivation it will usually be desired to incorporate some other principle, broadly representing need, in the operation. This can still be achieved by direct revenue transfer, for instance by what is known as the Distributable Pool method.[1] Predetermined percentages of certain tax revenues are paid into a pool. The contents of this are then allocated percentagewise to the states on a predetermined basis. The whole operation is determined by an independent Commission, taking account of such factors as derivation and needs (measured by population).[2] The weights given to these are not revealed, but provision is made for adjustment by another independent Commission after five years.

The advantages of the Distributable Pool method are, first, that the states will have some broad idea of what is coming to them over a period, and secondly that there is no excuse for the national government not to make the correct distribution, since the revenue will already be in its hands. Third, and more important, price changes do not affect the formula since it is set in percentage terms. Against these must be set two decided disadvantages. In the first place revenue fluctuations are directly transmitted to the states so that in practice any firm forward planning is ruled out. Secondly the formula makes no allowance for changing relative circumstances of the states. In a development country these may be very substantial over a period of five years. Moreover succeeding Commissions will have much more difficulty in making suitable adjustments than if the statistical basis of the weighting were made clear. In fact experience shows that development countries do not long remain satisfied with this secret allocation.

Revenue allocation through a distributable pool in practice very closely approximates to a block or unallocated grant; the main difference being that with the pool system the total to be

1. This method was adopted in India, the Federation of Rhodesia and Nyasaland, Nigeria, and (for the Common Services) East Africa, all on the advice of Sir Jeremy Raisman.

2. Two further factors are stated to have been considered by the Raisman Commission in Nigeria: (i) continuity, (ii) funds required to perform statutory obligations properly. The first of these cannot be interpreted strictly if adjustments are ever to be made. The second could be subsumed under 'needs'.

distributed depends on fiscal experience, whereas the total of a grant would no doubt be fixed for a period, although successive annual quotes could be allowed to rise to leave room for growth. It must be presumed that the formula in which the grant is based would be made known, and preferably discussed with the units.[1] This implies that more consideration would have to be given to the factors to be included and to their respective weights; although no doubt the general framework would still be a compromise between derivation and needs.

It is usual to give a substantial weight to population on the argument that service costs are broadly proportionate to the population to be served. If too much weight is put on this factor, however, there are two difficulties. First, until there is adequate registration of births and deaths population figures may be very inaccurate. Censuses can get distorted by various causes: under recording because of fear of taxation, inflation to gain political advantage. (Both of these factors have clearly operated in Nigeria.) Secondly, population may be very unevenly distributed. Some services are more expensive to run when the population is sparse; exceptional density also gives rise to special requirements of training and emigration. It may be desirable to add some weighting for these.[2] Further, it may be desirable to give special assistance not only at the start, but continually, for diseconomies of administration due to small scale, if the units cannot be amalgamated (for instance small islands). On rare occasions it may be possible to get estimates of unit G.D.P.'s. Provided these are the work of the federal statistical office or of an independent body such as a university research unit,[3] they can be of great value in drawing up a rational grant system.

If it is desired to put substantial emphasis on uniformity of services a superficially attractive device is to award deficiency grants to units which cannot balance their current budgets without help. This method has been followed in India for some years in respect of Union grants to states. It is also the basis of grants in aid from the British Treasury to the smaller Caribbean islands.

---

1. In the U.K. general (unallocated) grants for local authorities are only determined by the government after prolonged discussion with the associations of local authorities.

2. Both of these factors figure in the British General Grant.

3. Thus in the Caribbean island G.D.P.'s have been calculated by the University. cf. Report of Fiscal Commission, 1963.

Deficiency grants which are not carefully looked after may go seriously wrong in two directions. The more active grant receivers take the opportunity to push into the current budget items which properly belong to the capital account and thus enlarge their grant. The more passive units cease to bother to collect their own taxes adequately, and so also enlarge their deficit. Consequently the grant giving government will be wise to lay down very carefully just in what form the budget accounts must be kept and what items may be included in the current account. If this is done adequately a good deal of frustrating detailed control can be avoided. The Australian Grants Commission seems to have solved this problem very successfully, and it is notable that its decisions seem to give general satisfaction. There are several reasons for supposing that the necessary combination of objectivity and sympathy can more easily be exercised by an independent commission than by a government department.

Unconditional grants have the very important advantage that they leave state budgeting unfettered, and, as we have seen, a substantial measure of equalisation can be written into the formulae. But a constructive grant policy will also call for some specific conditional grants, on the one hand to promote the development of basic national services, on the other as a means of control of the standard of services provided. It is however not desirable that specific grants should occupy a predominant place in the grant structure. They are disequalising in the sense that only the richer authorities can afford to take them up fully; they also distort state budgets, since any service not grant-aided is thereby discriminated against.[1] For specific grants it is desirable to fix some objective basis which must be reached in order to qualify for grant, such as a percentage contribution to teachers' salaries above a minimum class size. The rate of grant which it will be necessary to give for a particular service in order to stimulate state activity depends very largely on the relative interest of the national and state governments in the service; the greater the state interest the smaller the grant need be. If desired a measure of equalisation can also be written into the formula for

---

1. It was for this reason that the Shoup Mission to Japan (Report on Japanese Taxation, 1949) recommended that specific grants should not exceed 18 per cent of the total of grants.

a specific grant;[1] but no grant should ever reach 100 per cent as this removes all incentive for good management on the part of the grant receiving government.

It emerges from this discussion that a grant structure can incorporate a very large number of factors, so that it can be tailored exactly to fit local circumstances; provided first that certain basic statistics are available, and secondly that the national government can be relied upon to honour its commitments. This is not so easy as it sounds;[2] much depends on the amount that has to be transferred in grants relative to the size of its own budget. This is particularly important in the case of specific grants based on an objective formula, since they are essentially 'open-ended' so far as the national government is concerned. It is under obligation to aid all expenditure which passes the necessary tests. Grants are also extremely flexible; but care must be taken to see that they are not so flexible that they destroy the basis for forward planning. The size of the grants should be known by the states in advance for a definite period. A minimum for this is probably three years.

This last proposition implies that lower layer government will be able (and should be encouraged) to take an active part in economic development. Although because of their limited resources even state governments in a federation[3] cannot usually be expected to undertake very large projects, there is no doubt that national progress will be quicker the more widely based is the interest and co-operation in development. Nevertheless the national plan is clearly more important than any given state plan. The national government must also take responsibility for the co-ordination of state plans. These are matters which we shall have to discuss in the next chapter; here we are only concerned with meeting the costs of development and their distribution between different levels of government.

Generally speaking it should be possible to finance small works

1. The first British grant to incorporate an equalisation element was the Education Grant (from 1914), the equalisation being obtained by the deduction of the product of a penny rate when the objective elements had been totalled. This helped authorities the product of whose penny rate was low.

2. I found in 1964 that the faces of all the Nigerian Regions were set against grants, which otherwise would have been desired, owing to the federal government having failed to make some that it had promised.

3. Nigeria is an exception, since there the federal plan is virtually limited to its own services and to development in the federal territory of Lagos.

with little or no help from central funds. It is sometimes convenient if the higher authority makes its contribution in kind: in
cement, steel girders, corrugated iron roof and so on. This saves
the pocket of the executing authority and enables the goods to
be economically purchased in bulk by the national government
when there are a number of projects to be financed. Another
method is for the higher level government to make grants in cash
according to a 'tariff' for different types of works, provided that
they conform to certain standards. In a development country it is
as well not to pay these over until there is clear evidence of
willingness and ability to complete. If the works are to be carried
out by urban authorities and the state in which they are situated
is itself very poor it may be advisable for the national government
to make a grant to the executing authority *through* the state;
this method is increasingly used in India. Where the works are
to be financed out of loan an alternative type of aid is for the
national government to give an annual grant to assist in servicing
the loan.[1]

Large projects naturally give rise to more difficulties. Here a
problem of strength of relative interests—national and state—
arises similar to the one we found in respect of grants. If the works
will be primarily of local or regional interest, such as an irrigation
scheme, the states concerned can properly be required to provide
a substantial share of the cost. If the interest is primarily national
or the location of the project is technically fixed in an awkward
place, or overlapping state boundaries, the national government
can reasonably shoulder a large part of the burden. In any case
it cannot be expected that assistance with capital works will fit
neatly into the general grant structure. They tend to be too large
and too irregular. Consequently the conditions under which aid
will be awarded need to be separately determined, probably on
the basis of the individual project.

Generally speaking larger projects will require a certain amount
of loan finance. As noted earlier, experience in the older federations
shows that if states have completely independent borrowing
powers some will tend to overborrow and get into difficulties.
In respect of domestic borrowing, where the balance of payments
is not involved, it is however reasonable to allow lower level

1. This has been the principle form of grant given by the central government
in the U.K. to finance the large programme of local authority low income
housing.

governments to raise some of their own funds locally, preferably by mortgage or other short loan, which will not interfere with national monetary control. As suggested in Chapter 3, the more opportunities are made available to potential lenders, the larger is likely to be the volume of savings generated. In respect of the larger loans, however, there is much to be said for a policy of centralised borrowing on behalf of the states, either through the central bank or through a public agency such as a Loans Board. The former method is extensively used in India, although it is not compulsory; the latter has been used especially successfully in Kenya, where the granting of loans to local authorities is made to depend on the attainment of sound budgetary practices and adequate reserves.

External borrowing is in a different class; it clearly comes within the—usually exclusive—province of the national government because of the direct relevance of debt service to the balance of payments. However, because the total volume of loans must be centrally controlled, there is no reason why there should be any detailed control over their application, and perhaps not even over their location. Australia has for some decades employed the services of an independent Loans Board on which both the Commonwealth and state governments are represented. It is not certain however that such a body would give more satisfaction in a development country where planning is a very high priority. In any case the Loans Board would have to keep in very close and continuous touch with the planners. These are points with which we can deal more conveniently in the next chapter.

CHAPTER SEVEN

THE ORGANISATION AND EXECUTION OF DEVELOPMENT PLANS

1. *The Stages of Plan Organisation*

IN this chapter we shall be concerned with general principles. We shall not attempt to cover the technical and physical aspects of planning, but shall rather explore the fiscal and monetary implications of period planning, seen as a large additional exercise which must be carried out against the background of the normal activities of the public sector and of the transactions of the other sectors of an economy. Naturally the content of plans and their fiscal implications will differ substantially from country to country, depending on such factors as natural resources and the degree of development already attained when planning begins. Nevertheless the principles to be observed, and the pitfalls to be guarded against, have sufficient generality to be applicable to a wide range of economic and political circumstances.

The general aim of policy must be to ensure that development takes place smoothly, without stops and starts, either in particular projects (bearing in mind that projects will be related to each other both economically and technically), or in the whole process of Plan implementation. Projects which remain half finished for months or even years are a waste in themselves and prevent the employment of resources in productive ways. In order to secure an even flow of development two conditions are of overriding importance. First, the Plan must be internally consistent, so that one part supports and does not frustrate another. Secondly, it must be within the capacity of the economic resources over which the government has command or which it can reasonably look forward to having at its disposal over the Plan period. A broad correspondence between resources and demands on them is not sufficient, although it is a useful start. The factors which go into different projects are by no means fully interchangeable. It is necessary sooner or later to plan individually with the particular needs of the different works and services in mind. There is, however, a good deal to be said for starting at the global or macro-economic end.

The first step in planning would be consequently what is sometimes called 'appraisal of potentialities'. The developments which it is (broadly) desired to see included in the Plan (either because they appear to be particularly promising economically or particularly essential from the social point of view) need to be measured up against the total of production and its distribution as revealed in the national accounts,[1] both at the initial point and as projected over the Plan period. The 'notional total' for Plan outlay (which is all that can be foreseen at this stage) has to find its place alongside the needs of existing provisions in the established services, bearing in mind that their demands will be expanding all the time, due to 'creep'[2] even in the absence of rising costs. Further, sufficient room has to be left for consumption and investment outside the government sector: in other parts of the public sector, such as state and local government activities, in nationalised industries, and above all for anticipated consumption and investment in the private sector. The rate of development will tend to be slowed up if the legitimate expectations of the private sector are disappointed, either in respect of production (so that full advantage cannot be taken of the opportunities provided by the public sector) or in consumption. Disappointment in respect of promises of availability of goods and services breeds discontent and perhaps unwillingness to co-operate fully in the development process.

For operational use the national accounts need to be as complete and detailed as possible. The aim should be to recalculate them year by year. It is not, however, the total that is of first importance, and, as we shall see shortly, there are conceptual as well as statistical difficulties in reaching an unambiguous figure for the G.N.P. of a development country. The key factor on which the planners need to concentrate is the intersectoral flow of payments between the public sector with its various outliers, the business and productional sector, the domestic sector, and above all, the rest-of-the-world sector. Within the business sector the finer the breakdown that can be made between different industries and investments the more helpful will it be for forecasting. It is also very desirable to encourage the statisticians to make direct estimates of

1. For a simple account of the general principles of national accounting see J. R. Hicks, *The Social Framework*, Ch. 16.

2. See above, p. 6. Sometimes called 'escalation' but this includes higher rates of pay.

'capital consumption'—the wearing out of fixed capital and the running down of stocks and stores—even rather rough direct estimates are preferable to inferring changes in these items as residuals.

If, or as soon as, data allow it is extremely useful to attempt an input/output table, showing the additional inputs of labour and equipment necessary to secure a given expansion of output in different directions. This will serve as a check on the interrelation of different economic activities and their respective demands on resources. If sufficient data can be made available (and statistical expertise allows) a symbolic model can be made for the whole economy, incorporating the input/output technique for forecasting resource requirements.[1] Such a model serves as a most valuable check that due attention has been paid to all the relevant variables.

It is naturally desirable that the model should be as realistic as possible so that it should take account of whatever constraints and boundaries the decision makers determine to impose on the planners' plans. By means of such a model it is possible to set precise expansion targets. The model can thus serve both as a guide to balance in the Plan and as an indication of the order of magnitude of feasible growth with the given resources. At present the statistics of most development countries do not allow of such refined exercises; but awareness of future possibilities can even now lead to better planning, if only by the stimulus it gives to the improvement of statistics.

The setting of targets is an important stage in the planning process because they give publicity and so focus the interest of the public, while at the same time they act as a spur to Ministers and administrators. At this stage it is useful for public relations to display the broad forecast of development in the public sector over the Plan period. This should be set out in a very simple form so that all will be able to appreciate the plans of the government. For purposes of comparison the table should be drawn up at the prices ruling at the beginning of the exercise, notwithstanding the fact that there may be substantial changes over the period; for this is not a costing account. The purposes of the table are, first, to give the order of magnitude of the total, which can then be

---

1. cf. H. M. Phillips, 'International Aid for Educational Development in the form of technical assistance and real resources', *Papers of the Conference on the Economics of Education*, International Economic Association, 1963.

checked against the projected G.N.P., and secondly and more importantly, to display the relative magnitudes of the various services and their projected expansion.[1]

As already mentioned, a serious obstacle, which is both conceptual and statistical, lies in the path of attempts to estimate the G.N.P. of a development country for operational purposes; this is due to the large agricultural sector. It is almost impossible to get a firm figure of output, more especially of that part which still lies in the subsistence sector. For the estimation of inter-sectoral flow, however, the sector which is still engaged in subsistence production is not a great importance. Subsistence production is almost wholly unplanned and its sectoral flow to and from other parts of the economy is minimal. Consequently its reaction to government policy will be extremely sluggish. For planning purposes it may be less misleading to omit it completely than to attempt to ascribe a value to its contribution. The more normal case, however, is the farm family whose production and consumption are partly subsistence, but which makes sales and purchases in the money sector. These latter will of course be

1. A table of the following form should suffice (cf. The Long Term Forecast of British Public Expenditure, in Cmd. 2235 of 1963: cit).

TABLE I (£ ('000 OMITTED) AT COMMENCEMENT PRICES)

	1965/6	%	1969/70	%	Increase Decrease ±	%
Defence						
Overseas representation						
Education						
Health & Welfare						
Housing & Environmental services						
Police and justice						
Assistance to Industry, Agriculture & Transport						
Communications						
Investment in Nationalised industries etc.						
Administration						
Contingencies						
TOTAL		100		100		Average

valued at market prices (so far as they can be ascertained), but there is no satisfactory answer to the problem of valuing their subsistence output (which incidentally often includes a substantial amount of investment in farm improvements). To count this at market prices gives an overvaluation, since if all had been sold the price structure would probably have been different. Yet to count it at 'cost' gives an undervaluation.[1] What is important, however, is not the value of the subsistence output, but the margin of change between the subsistence and the market economy, in terms of supplies and demands on the market and of labour movement.

Having performed the preliminary operation of appraisal of potentialities, the share of the country's resources which can be devoted to the Plan depends in the first place on the type of plan which it is desired to use. The possible variations of type are infinite, but it will suffice for our purposes to distinguish three mai nvarieties. First, a plan may consist of a few individual projects, chosen presumably because they are themselves deemed to be of paramount importance or to constitute bottlenecks in the way of further development. This is a very simple form of planning, with which it may be possible to get by without much statistical apparatus, so long as the projects are not large enough to exert immediate general effects within the economy or in the balance of payments.

2. *Shopping Lists and Plans*

If the projects are few and not very large (taking the form, for instance, of a rice mill here and a paper factory there), even the local effect will be negligible and the overspill will consequently be zero. On the other hand if the projects are large and numerous enough to realise overspill they will amount to a 'shopping list' plan—a series of disconnected projects put in hand without any clear relation one to another. Large shopping list plans which are

1. To value the yams which the farmer produces and consumes at the price at which he would buy yams (in the city) is to put too high a price on them; he does not do that because he can produce them more cheaply. To value them at the price at which he could sell them is to set too low a price; he does not sell them because they are worth more to him for direct consumption than he could get by selling them to anyone else. The trouble with subsistence farming is that the gap between buying and selling price is abnormally wide.

not measured up against available resources lead straight to balance of payments troubles. Nevertheless if well chosen the individual project plan can pave the way for general growth. Such was the first Monnet plan in France, concentrating on heavy industry, especially steel, in which France had previously lagged behind most of her neighbours. It must be recalled, however, that during the years of greatest strain in implementing the Plan the franc was stoutly supported by the dollar; nevertheless it was found necessary eventually to devalue the franc heavily.

The succession of Five Year Plans in India are typical of a second variety of planning. The Indian plan is in principle a fully integrated and comprehensive programme for the Union government sector. It broadly takes into account the individual plans of the states, and joint execution of projects common to the Union and a state government figure in it. Some effort has been made to put the Plan in the background of the national accounts, but the statistics do not allow of a very close consistency. Some of the activities of the private sector, both in industry and agriculture, are, however, more or less directly controlled by the government—for instance in respect of permitted exports or sales on the home market. There has been much less control of consumption and this has been one factor contributing to balance of payments difficulties. Implementation of large projects is generally in the hands of foreign firms or consortia. That the Indian plans have not been more successful in raising per capita income is not primarily due to inherent weakness in planning (except in so far as insufficient attention has been paid to the financial side and to the activities of the private sector). Their limited success is overwhelmingly due to the population explosion and to the lack of reliable rains to support agricultural output. In the absence of the plans, however, there is no doubt that the situation would have been very much worse; per capita income could well have fallen quite substantially.

Recent French four year plans are typical of the third variety of planning.[1] This is in one sense the most comprehensive type of planning yet attempted in a mixed economy, and it is no accident that it has been typical of advanced rather than of development countries. It certainly seems that French planning has been a success. A high growth rate has been maintained, coupled with a

---

1. Present British policy seems to be following along similar lines.

very strong balance of payments, and only moderate inflationary pressure. This sort of plan embraces the whole economy, but so far as production in the private sector is concerned it operates by persuasion, not by compulsion. So far as consumption in the private sector is concerned, control in the interests of stability has been exercised almost wholly through the fiscal system, in particular by means of the Tax on Value Added, with a small amount of support from credit control. This slender defence against inflation has probably only worked because weak trade union organisation has on the whole not succeeded in pushing up wages to compensate for the operation of the T.V.A. in raising prices.

The interesting thing about French planning[1] is its technique. This depends on two factors which would only gradually become available in a development country. Nevertheless some adaptation of the procedure might even now be possible in particular sectors. The first factor is a planning unit[2] backed by a large secretariat of high grade economic statisticians. The second is a body of industrialists (with some trade unionists) who are capable of estimating with considerable precision both production and marketing possibilities in their own lines, once they are given (a) a projected growth rate for the economy as a whole, on which to base their forecasts, and (b) an assurance that labour and materials necessary for the appropriate expansion in their own industries will be available.[3] It must not be overlooked that it is essential for the working of the system that there is already in existence a developed infrastructure of fuel, power and communications on the one hand and on the other a standard of education and training which enables industrial labour to be easily mobile between occupations.

The first step in French planning is to determine the feasible growth rate for the economy as a whole, to which the individual industrial expansion rates can be tied. (They will naturally differ from one industry to another.) Since the largest outlet for sales is likely to be the home market, accurate forecast of domestic

1. It is unnecessary to go into detail here because a vast literature on the subject is now available, especially J. and A. N. Hackett, *Economic Planning in France*, Allen and Unwin, 1963, and P. Bauchet, *Economic Planning, the French Experience*, Heinemann, 1964.

2. Commissariat du Plan.

3. There is also a general Economic Council, supposedly advisory, but in practice of little importance.

consumers' demand is vital for French planning. This is a potential weakness, but so far seems to have been amenable to control
through appropriate adjustments in the rates of the T.V.A. (which
at one time operated with fourteen different rates). The next
step is to analyse in detail the required inputs for each industry in
order to reach its target. This is a co-operative exercise, undertaken jointly by representatives of the industry[1] working in
collaboration with a section of the central Plan Commissariat
detailed to it. The final stage is to integrate section plans into a
whole, which is then checked for consistency and feasibility.
Once the Plan has been hammered into the required shape through
this process it is unlikely that the government will reject it. Moreover, once the authorities have sanctioned a particular growth
rate for an industry they are under some obligation to see that the
necessary inputs are available. There is no such commitment for
production in excess of the Plan and the manufacturer will be left
to his own devices; he is unlikely to stray far.

It would be open for a development country to choose in principle any of these varieties of planning. On the whole it is most
likely to opt for the Indian variety as being best adapted to
nation building.

Operational plans in development countries run for a varied
number of years; but there is a general consensus of opinion that
five is about right. If a longer span is chosen, in a rapidly changing
world, economic parameters may alter so drastically as to make
a number of the targets inappropriate. If a much shorter period is
chosen it can only be expected to reach a few worthwhile targets,
or to complete only a small number of projects within the period.
While successive plans are of necessity closely integrated over
time and cannot sensibly be considered in isolation, it is more
satisfactory to have some definite stage of achievement to con-
template by the final year of a plan period. In addition to an operational period plan it is also useful to look ahead in 'perspective'
over three or four plan periods, in order to steer the economy on a
broadly charted course. The perspective plan can also be given
targets, such as the establishment of free primary education of a
certain standard, proportion of primary children passing into
secondary school, additional provision of electric power, and above

---

1. For the Fourth Plan there were 22 Vertical and 5 Horizontal Commissions.
The former have to do with 'activities'—usually industrial groupings—the
latter with matters that concern more than one activity, such as research.

all an estimate of the improvement in the per capita income over the period. It is, however, dangerous to regard such perspective plans as operational. Even if they are fulfilled they may lead to a pattern of investment which, owing to unforeseeable factors, turns out to be non-optimal.

Whatever is done about perspective planning it is quite essential to have frequent re-appraisals of programming of the Plan projects. This is partly to check that the projects and programmes are working out as well as was anticipated, and partly to evaluate the progress since the last review. It is frequently the practice not to hold such a review until the Plan period is half way through; this is doubtfully soon enough, as many things can go awry in two and a half years. An annual review is decidedly to be preferred, even if there is little to record in the first year. It should be noted however that annual re-appraisal of a period plan is not the same thing as year to year planning without a longer period frame of reference, even though the exercise may be related to current national income statistics. In the guise of flexibility such year to year 'planning' tends to lead to 'piecemeal commitments':[1] more projects are sanctioned than can be completed at an optimum rate of implementation, due to physical and financial limitations. If the commitments have been assumed within a national accounting framework the result will be stoppages and cut backs. If no adequate account has been taken of available resources, inflationary pressure and balance of payments troubles will probably ensue.

3. *Machinery for Plan Organisation*

We must next consider the administrative and executive set up required for Plan organisation and implementation. Individual circumstances, especially on the political side, may differ very much in this respect so that it would be rash to postulate a unique answer. It must be borne in mind that every project needs to go through four successive stages: (i) feasibility assessment (ii) detailed costing (iii) implementation and (iv) evaluation. Bodies need to be available to take responsibility for these severally. Their organisation might be as follows. First, a Planning Unit at the professional—(career) level, including the best economists

1. This is the phrase used by the Plowden Committee on the Control of Public Expenditure in the U.K., 1961.

and statisticians that can be collected; secondly a Planning Board at the Ministerial level, with a competent secretariat. The work of these two would mainly be related to the two first of the above processes. Next would come a body which might be designated the National Development Board, to co-ordinate responsibility for implementation and evaluation. A number of countries have also established a National Economic Council[1] with high sounding names but acting only in an advisory capacity, which meets perhaps twice a year and whose usefulness is mainly as a policy-making body in a very broad sense. The functions of the three working bodies described above are separate and distinct. How far it is necessary for the personnel also to be distinct would, however, depend on the scale of operations. At a regional or state planning level the simpler the organisation the better, so long as the separate functions are adequately looked after. We must now go into these in a little more detail.[2]

The Planning Unit should probably be attached to the Ministry of Finance, but could function equally well under the aegis of the Cabinet or Prime Minister's Office. It would be a mistake to give it any less central position; but in practice it should have a good deal of independence. Its main duties would be to assist and co-ordinate on the global basis of the Plan as a whole; but it must also be prepared to assist with the preparation of individual projects. The relevant Ministries would be responsible for technical aspects, but they would not be able to command economic expertise. The Planning Unit could not be expected to possess as high a degree of technical competence but would supply the economic checks, in particular cost consciousness at all stages. In a federation the central planning unit may find itself in a somewhat anomalous position and if state rights are firmly entrenched will have to walk very carefully. As we have argued, it is important for lower layer governments to be drawn into the planning process as fully as

1. The Indian National Development Council for instance consists of the Prime Minister, Plan chiefs, state Chief Ministers, and Ministers of all spending Departments. It meets every 5–6 months. It makes no decisions but passes resolutions.

2. I must here acknowledge the stimulus I have derived from L. J. Walinsky's little book, *The Planning and Execution of Economic Development*, McGraw-Hill, 1963. Mr. Walinsky writes from practical experience of plan execution in various parts of the developing world. His experience supplements (and largely confirms) conclusions I have reached from observation of plan content and implementation in a fairly wide range of countries, but with a somewhat different coverage from Mr. Walinsky's.

possible so long as they do not do anything to impede national progress. Some of them may have fairly ample funds at their disposal but they are unlikely to be able to command the necessary expertise for effective planning. Hence the central planning unit has an overriding responsibility to see that state plans are adequate.

As examples of the different federal/state relations in respect of planning which may be workable, we may cite India, Nigeria and the Caribbean among the development countries. In India the central Planning Commission is extremely powerful and has always been closely in touch with the Prime Minister. On the other hand while some of the states are eager and effective planners others are indifferent, some through poverty, some probably because South Indians do not take kindly to what they regard as interference from Delhi. However, as Indian finances are, for a federation, rather exceptionally centralised the central planning unit is able, with Parliamentary sanction, to secure the fulfilment of what it deems necessary by means of generous grant aid. The central Planning Commission sends a deputation to interview state planning officers and discuss their plans, at least once a year. But the latter will emphasize that they can only be persuaded, not driven.

In Nigeria planning in the Regions has always had priority, with initially the federal government confining its plans to its own services; especially electricity supply, railways, trunk roads and the coal mines, apart from the development of the federal Territory of Lagos. This arrangement was found to give insufficient liaison between Federal and Regional plans. A National Planning Committee has now been formed which does the effective work. Conferences of financial secretaries and planners are held about once a month, in the Regional and federal capitals in rotation. In addition there is a Central Economic Council which meets about twice a year, and is more effective than these things often are. Regional and federal plans are thus now co-ordinated, but the federal government is tending to play an increasingly important part in financing. (In the 1962/68 Plan the federal share of finance is estimated to be as high as 61 per cent. of the total. This, however, is largely accounted for by the exceptionally large cost of the Niger dam at Kainji for which the federal government has guaranteed over 30 per cent. of the finance.) In Nigeria the federal government does not command sufficient funds to exercise control through grants as the Indian government does, but (as we saw in the last chapter) it has in practice complete control of borrowing. Internal borrowing is centralised by the consent of the Regions, in order to avoid competition for scarce resources, but there have been a number of complaints of the federal government's arbitrary allocation of loan funds among the Regions. It would seem that Nigeria would be well advised to introduce more formal machinery for the purpose, such as a modified version of the Australian Loans Board, but with rather more central authority.

The Caribbean is another area where the independent rights of the Units are jealously guarded; but it is out of the question for the smaller islands to command the necessary expertise for effective planning. The London Conference of 1962, which drew up general lines on which a federation of the Eastern islands might (and may yet) work, was consequently recognising the inevitable, as well as the optimal, in voting for a strong central planning unit. The functions of this would be more to help the islands with their own plans than to impose any overriding blue print for the area. It could, however, play a very useful part in restraining over-investment in certain lines, notably tourism.

These various federal experiences show, as is only to be expected, that the more complex form of government complicates the planning process. Generally speaking some of the most awkward problems in federal finance are related to the difficulty of securing steady growth with disseminated decision making. It will not be surprising if the national influence in planning tends relatively to expand.

The Ministerial Planning Board would include the Ministers of all Departments involved in the execution of plans, and, obviously, the Minister of Finance. It would be chaired by the Prime Minister, or, in a country with an executive President, by the President himself. The Board's main duty would be to fill in the details of the government's broad policy decisions. It would naturally be possible for the Cabinet itself to act in lieu of a separate Planning Board. This is not likely to be successful, however, for two reasons. In the first place some members whose Ministries were not directly concerned with development would be more or less passengers, and at the best would contribute little and might well be obstructive. Secondly, the chance of party politics entering to the detriment of economic considerations would be much greater. This danger is particularly serious in a one-party government where there can be no effective opposition to challenge and criticise government decisions.

The Planning Board, like the Planning Unit, would, as we have seen, be mainly concerned with the first two stages of project processing and co-ordination, both within the Plan and in relation to the total activities of the public sector. The National Development Board would have the special duty of looking after the remaining stages, of implementation and evaluation, with particular emphasis on implementation, or execution, which is the key stage of the whole process. There is no reason why there should not be a good deal of overlapping in personnel between the Planning Board and the Development Board. The latter would include both Ministers and heads of Executive Agencies of projects for which a Ministry was not itself the executive body. It would also need to include some top civil servants, especially the Permanent Secretary of the Ministry of Finance. The Board would need to meet frequently in order to keep in touch with the working out of all projects; but it would clearly have to delegate the actual work of execution control. We must return to this point in a moment.

4. *Choice and Processing of Projects*

It will be remembered that in Chapter 2 we discussed the principles which should underlie the choice of projects. Proposals for projects to be included in the Plan may emanate from a number of sources. Policy programmes already accepted, such as the establishment of an educational pyramid of a particular shape, will in turn imply works and plans of a particular type. The impulse for these would be at Cabinet level, the Planning Unit's main concern being to proffer advice on cost/benefit lines. Other proposals are likely to come from the Planning Unit itself, since from its co-ordinating position it will best be able to perceive gaps in programmes, or policy decisions that carry within them the seeds of imbalance. Probably most proposals, however, are likely to emanate from one or other of the executive Ministries.

In addition to the examination of suggested projects by the Planning Unit, it would be the responsibility of the Development Board to iron out in good time political differences, including the relative claims of different Ministries, several of whom may consider that a particular project belongs to their jurisdiction. Commissions of Enquiry in advanced countries have repeatedly drawn attention to the waste caused by several Ministries[1] trying to do the same job. Not all of this overlapping is due to ignorance of what other Ministries are doing. In a development country when most of the Ministries (and Ministers) are new on the job, confusion is likely to be still greater.[2] It is most important that all these difficulties should be straightened out before heavy costs are incurred.

We now come to the processing of a project which has been passed for inclusion in the Plan. The Planning Unit will now have to work very closely with the Ministry responsible for implementation. This Ministry will have to consider the new project in relation to the programmes on which it is already engaged; but it is by no means necessary for the Ministry itself to undertake the actual execution. It may be more satisfactory either to establish an *ad hoc* Agency for the purpose, which would be less bound by routine control and would consequently find it easier to engage the necessary specialists. Alternatively, if the project is a large one, it may be better to turn execution over to a foreign concern or consortium with good experience in that particular line.

Whatever the selected method of execution, the Ministry concerned must necessarily retain its responsibility to the Planning Unit and the government for the proper execution of the project. This responsibility extends over all the four phases of processing; at these we must now take a somewhat closer look. The first step, feasibility appraisal, is mainly concerned with physical factors. For instance, it is desired to construct a deep water harbour in a shallow lagoon. It is necessary to ascertain the best trace for a canal, to find out whether rock blasting will be required and whether the tides and winds will make it impossible to prevent silting up. (This example comes from Antigua.) Again, it is proposed to start a paper factory, in order to utilise a certain wild grass which chemical analysis has shown to be suitable for making high grade paper. The first necessity is to ensure that an ample supply of the raw material will be regularly available, sufficient to provide for continuous full capacity working. Equally important is to explore in advance how and where the product will be marketed. (This example comes from Ceylon. In the event the supply of grass quickly

1. For instance the Committee on National Expenditure in the U.K. in the 1920's, and the Plowden Committee on the Control of Expenditure, 1961.

2. An unfortunate example from India is the overlapping of the Ministry of Health and the Ministry of Community Development in Delhi; several Committees have recommended their merger.

gave out and the factory could only be kept going on imported material, for the delivery of which the siting was highly inconvenient.) Examples of this type could be multiplied indefinitely in the development countries.

If there are no local experts capable of evaluating feasibility it will be advisable to engage a firm of foreign consultants; in any case it is useful to have the additional assurance of experience. (If the World Bank is interested in the project it will look after all this side.) This is the stage also at which the objectives of the project need careful definition in order to eliminate inconsistency or ambivalance. Almost every country in the world is guilty of ambivalance in its plans, especially in its agricultural programmes: employment, land settlement, cheap food for consumers, good profits for farmers, and additional exports, jostle each other for prior consideration. Once the main objective has been defined the others will either be shown to be inconsistent or will take their place as overspill, additional, objectives. A point which is frequently overlooked is the importance of location of projects for which there is no overriding technical position. A bad location can easily ruin a good project and prevent it having a proper overspill effect. Advanced countries, whether mixed or controlled economies, endemically suffer from the interference of politics in location. In development countries the danger of mislocation is still greater because the new governments are themselves weak and must endeavour to placate important supporters.

Elaborate costing is not called for until the feasibility of a project has been thoroughly investigated. It is desirable, however, to have an early, even if very broad, estimate of total costs and benefits, including the most obvious overspill effects. The detailed costing process is exacting, and here the Planning Unit will need decisively to take the lead. This is the stage at which it is most likely to be possible to quantify cost/benefit analysis between alternative techniques to reach the agreed objective.[1] As we saw in Chapter 2, the cost/benefit technique requires that alternative streams of costs and benefits are discounted to the present at the previously chosen social time preference rate, (representing the government's view of the correct balance of present and future in the interests of the citizens it serves.) If it is hoped to get a grant or soft loan for a project this will figure as a reduction in the cost

1. In the terminology of Chapter 2, at the fourth level of choice.

stream, but will not do anything directly to move the project to a higher priority.[1]

The commonest pitfall in the costing process is the failure to allow sufficiently for complementary and supplementary costs implied in a decision to proceed with a project, more especially if it appears that a good bargain is being offered by a foreign country. Land commonly costs more than anticipated; supplementary fixed capital may be required immediately, by way of roads, housing, pipe lines and whatever else is required to permit full capacity working. There must also be provision for replacement; especially of mechanical equipment which does not stand up well to inexpert handling in tropical climates. Working capital and running costs include stocks and spares and such items as school furniture and books, hospital furniture and drugs. Like the fixed capital they all require to be maintained. Finally provision needs to be made for personnel of the right skills and in balanced proportions, and for their increasing costliness, year by year. These are matters to which we shall have to return in the next chapter.

5. *Plan Integration and Implementation*

The next step is to integrate the separate projects into a Plan, the notional total for this having already been given, in relation to the needs of continuing services and of permissible expansion as revealed by the national accounts. No doubt there will be some give and take in all this; the notional total is not final. Putting the Plan together is the most important responsibility which the Planning Unit has to undertake. It will need, however, to keep in constant touch with the Ministry of Finance, not only in respect of the demands of the rest of the economy, but because this Ministry will have the best knowledge concerning supplies of capital funds likely to be available from home or abroad. It is useful at this stage to work out a Chart (see Table 2) which shows at a glance (read across) the contribution of the various projects included in the Plan: whether to social overheads, economic overheads or to final output, and at the same time (read downwards) the economic character of the investment inputs required, distinguishing carefully those that will have to be imported.[2]

---

1. Reports by the World Bank's experts on projects in which it is interested now provide a useful model on how to put forecasts together.

2. A broadly similar table appears in Manual for Economic and Functional Classification of Government Transactions, U.N. 1958.

TABLE 2

CENTRAL GOVERNMENT DEVELOPMENT OUTLAYS BY
ECONOMIC CONTRIBUTION AND CHARACTER

Estimates relate to
year 196x

Appropriations relate to
the previous year 196x-1

Contribution → / Character ↓	Infrastructure		Superstructure Final Output
	Social overheads	Economic overheads	
	Education/Health/ Housing/ Domestic water, &c.	Communications/Ports/ Water/Basic agricultural improvement/ Tech. Education/ Research, &c.	Industry, Agriculture, Hydro-electric, Tourism, &c.
Purchase of Goods and Services for Development.			
1. Land			
2. Works and Buildings. *Import Requirements*			
3. Machinery and Equipment. *Import Requirements*			
4. Stores and Spares. *Import Requirements*			
5. Labour Skilled Unskilled *Import Requirements*			
Total New Investment			

The economic character of the inputs is important since they will have different multiplier and other effects, according to their nature. Such a chart is useful initially to check the balance of the Plan. Repeated year by year it will help to indicate to what extent balance as planned is being maintained. These are matters which we shall be discussing further in the next chapter.

While this Chart is intended mainly as a record of the central planning authority's outlay, it cna usefully be supplemented by a parallel account of investments by other layers of government, so far as they can be obtained. As we have seen these can be substantially influenced by grants and loans. The activities of public Agencies established to promote investment in the private sector can be similarly treated. As we have seen, most countries find that the establishment of an Industrial Development Corporation greatly increases the rate of private investment. A Tourist Board performs a similar task where there are genuine tourist possibilities. Finally an Agricultural Development Corporation will perform the same services for agriculture, both for large scale (plantation) and for small scale farmers. The functions of the first two of these bodies are, first, to attract firms, possibly enter into partnership with them and perhaps (but sparingly) make actual grants; secondly, the duty of thoroughly investigating the antecedents and competence of would-be investors falls on these bodies.[1] If care over this had been more widely taken in the past much disappointment and waste would have been avoided. Like the National Development Board the I.D.C. must be prepared to delegate. When a substantial amount of industrialisation has taken place it will no longer be able to look after all the cases itself. It may then be useful to follow the French plan of establishing industry committees charged with the promotion and development of important industries.[2]

The Agricultural Development Corporation, although also concerned with the private sector, will probably not be so directly involved with foreign firms on the production side. Its first duty will be to promote increased productivtiy in agriculture, including animal husbandry, tree crops and, where appropriate, forestry

1. As Mr. Walinsky wisely remarks, it is essential to beware of would-be investors whose primary interest is to sell their own equipment and who have no experience of working with it.

2. Presumably the same idea lies behind the establishment of industrial committees in the U.K. ('little Neddies') for the 17 industries which are the special care of the National Economic Development Council (Neddy).

and fishing. For this purpose it will need to establish a great many local branches so that no farming community need be without advice and *executive* assistance. The A.D.C. will also be the link between farmers and whatever organisation has been established to purvey agricultural credit. The second and no less important function of the A.D.C. should be Marketing—either directly or through individual crop Marketing Boards. There is no doubt at all that much of the failure of output and exports to increase in development countries is due to the inability of ordinary farmers, first to make the necessary foreign contacts, and secondly to grade and process their crops so that they reach an acceptable standard.[1] It must always be borne in mind that world markets for all tropical crops are highly competitive; only the most efficient can hope to succeed.

The process of implementation or execution is a matter both of keeping the individual projects moving and of preserving the smooth balance of the Plan as it unfolds. As we are envisaging it these tasks would be the special responsibility of the National Development Board, although the actual work of implementation would be the duty of the Ministry or Agency concerned. The Planning Unit and the Ministry of Finance would also have to be brought in, in respect of the phasing of the different projects. These need to be integrated and fitted into resource availability over time, just as much as at any moment of time, (see next page). The Ministry responsible should obtain field reports at frequent intervals and forward them to the National Development Board for processing. A competent project reporting staff would be needed for this purpose to work under the Executive Secretary of the Board, who might be designated Implementation Officer. The Board itself would need to meet very often—once a week has been suggested[2]—to consider the processed field reports. It would also probably need to get a quarterly report from all executive Ministries on all projects under their charge. It is important that reporting should be a two way process, going right down to field officers, who will function much better if they realise that their activities are of real interest to the authorities, that praise will be accorded wherever it is due, but that equally incompetence and laziness will not go unnoticed. In all this the Board must be

1. For more extended discussion of these matters see my Report on the Eastern Caribbean, cit.
2. See Walinsky, op. cit., also for all this section.

recognised as having supreme authority; but it must play its part adequately; making definite decisions promptly when they have to be made and issuing directions clearly and simply.

In order to spread and maintain interest in Plan progress it will be advisable for the Board to report periodically to the Cabinet on the progress of individual projects. For this purpose a project Chart or Record on the lines of Table 3 has been found useful. It will be seen that (read downwards) the information tallies exactly with that on Table 2. In fact a table of Development Outlay would very largely be a summary of project charts. Read across, however, over the months (and years), a series of charts will provide a step by step record of progress and of the successive obstacles encountered. When the executive Ministry sends in its Report it should, of course, be required to state in detail the reasons for divergences from the original estimate.

There is a tendency in all countries for execution to lag behind the original estimates of timing. There are many reasons for this, but probably unforeseen difficulties in land acquisition are among the most important. The result is that initially there is under-spending, but ultimately costs will be inflated by the delay. This tendency is especially marked, and especially awkward, in develop-ment countries with their limited resources and lack of flexibility. Generally speaking fixed capital works have a fairly consistent time profile: starting with very moderate inputs while the site is prepared and preliminary orders given, then expanding rapidly to a peak, and suddenly falling off as construction is completed. As experience of projects of different types accumulates, it should be possible to make a projection at a fairly early stage—say when actual work on the site begins—of the probable time profile. This will not only provide an additional check on the timing of actual performance, but will enable the authorities to plan how they will redeploy the labour force and equipment engaged on construction as soon as it becomes free.

Once the new works are completed they will probably require a very much smaller labour force for operation than during the construction period. On the other hand the demand for resources will now be permanent, and it will be necessary to have supplies of local labour appropriately trained. Similarly it will be necessary to arrange in advance for the necessary supplies of fuel and power as well as for regular supplies of stocks and spares. Finally arrange-ments will have to be made for eventual replacement of fixed

TABLE 3

PROJECT CONSTRUCTION RECORD, PROJECT K, PERIOD JAN. TO DECEMBER 196x

Starting Date:

Outlay on Construction	(1) Already Spent Cumulative/ last year	(2) Outlay to Completion Original/Revised	(3) Physical Capacity[1]			(4) Date of Completion Original/Revised
			Original Total Estimate	Present Working	Revised Estimate	
TOTAL						
1. Land						
2. Works, Buildings						
Import Requirements						
3. Machinery etc.						
Import Requirements						
4. Working capital						
Import Requirements						
5. Labour						
Import Requirements						

1. i.e. in such terms as KW hours, hospital beds, miles of roads of specific quality.

capital. Even before the construction period is over the planners can reasonably ask the executive agency to start making notes about future requirements. As soon as possible the Development Board should call for an annual return of all such requirements at the same time as the Agency sends in the progress report. This might take the form of Table 4; its use will go far to ensure that resources will be available as they are wanted.

TABLE 4

PROJECT OPERATIONAL EXPENDITURE REQUIREMENTS,
PROJECT K ($£$s)

	First Estimate	Present[1] Operation	Full Operation	Technical Details
1. Fixed Capital machinery (repairs and replacements)				
2. Stocks & Stores				
3. Labour professional skilled unskilled				
4. Other (fuel, power, water etc.)				

1. This column is intended to allow for partial operation in advance of completion, as when an unfinished dam permits some electric generation, or one wing of a hospital can be used in advance of the completion of the whole.

As argued above, frequent, preferably annual, programming and planning adjustment is an essential part of implementation. It is convenient to time this review with the preparation of the budget, that is after about six months of the financial year have elapsed.[1] By that time enough experience of this year's operations should be available to form a good basis for next year's estimates. Annual Plan adjustment needs to be a combined operation by the Planning Unit, the Ministry of Finance and the Development Board; in fact it cannot successfully be accomplished without the co-operation of all three. Normally only minor adjustments will be necessary; but the situation may change quickly in a number of ways, both in respect of implementation difficulties and of the availability of finance. If there happens to be a big (exogenous or other) change, such as a sudden worsening of the terms of trade,

1. On the timing of the budgetary process, see below, pp. 157, 158, 162.

which could not be foreseen, it may be necessary to prune plans drastically. This operation must clearly be undertaken jointly by the three bodies; left to itself the Ministry of Finance would have little choice but to order uniform cuts all across the board. Such a step could not avoid being inefficient and might easily be disastrous. However, there should be information readily available pointing to the least damaging cuts. The original cost/benefit estimates, now reinforced by estimates revised by experience, project by project, will be invaluable.

6. *Evaluation of Completed Projects*

The ex-post evaluation of the efficiency of development is a process which usually receives far too little attention. This may partly be because it cannot be carried out effectively until some experience of working has been gained and teething troubles may be expected to be over. It may be suspected, however, that evaluation has been neglected because it was nobody's business. Once a project is launched it tends to pass out of the public eye. Moreover, in respect of some sorts of development, it is by no means easy to arrive at the right sort of criteria for a judgment. In respect of commercial ventures indeed there should be no difficulty: a factory should be working to capacity and making at least normal profits. If it is not, the data for a diagnosis (or post mortem) should not be hard to come by. An efficiency test is not so easy for a public utility. Costs of producing the service may be high due to uncontrollable factors or to difficulties connected with the small size of the market (for instance for telephones). Even so, modified commercial criteria should be useable. For full efficiency there must either be increased output per unit of input or the same output at lower cost.

The most difficult evaluation problems are posed by the social services, especially health and education. The efficiency of hospitals can be judged partly by their unit running costs, for instance in terms of 'patient bed nights', partly by their success in effecting cures (so long as the distribution of heavy and light cases among hospitals is not skewed). In the advanced countries a good deal of research has been done along these lines,[1] but not

1. Nearly 200 hospitals in the U.K. keep annual returns of unit costs; cf. the pioneer researches of M. S. Feldstein into the efficiency of the British National Health Service, especially 'Economic Analysis, Operational Research, and the National Health Service', *Oxford Economic Papers*, 1963.

all of it is applicable to more primitive conditions. There may well be, however, instances of glaring inefficiency which can be detected, such as high incidence of diseases caught in hospital through indifferent standards of cleanliness, improper charges made by nurses to patients for the performance of their regular duties, or thefts of furnishings and drugs through inefficient stores control. It should not be thought that advanced countries are immune from these or similar difficulties; but that is no reason why the development countries should not try to do better. We shall be further concerned with these problems when we discuss the control of expenditure.

Evaluation of the success of an education programme is in a different class, if it is attempted (as it should be) to judge quality, and more particularly above the primary level. A good school inspection staff is a long run objective, but neither the personnel nor the funds are likely to be at present available in development countries. Public examination results help, but factors such as the home background of the children, the distance to be travelled to school and the size of classes may make them misleading. Perhaps the best solution is for the government to enlist the services of a University Social Research Institute[1] in a series of sample surveys. Trained independent investigators are in a much better position to make a penetrating and balanced evaluation than a government department.

Other services present somewhat different problems of evaluation, and appropriate procedures need to be worked out. The point to emphasise is that unless this final stage in the processing of development projects is conscientiously undertaken, it is impossible to obtain the best results from the resources employed.

7. *The Pattern of Supporting Finance*

So far we have only indirectly been concerned with paying for development; in the next chapter it will be a major preoccupation. There is however, one matter which must be discussed in the present chapter because it is directly concerned with the organisation of the Plan: the optimum relation between taxation and borrowing as methods of finance. This depends on a number of factors, and particularly on the structure of the Plan itself—its

1. Such as I saw in progress at the East African Institute of Social and Economic Research, Makerere, in the autumn of 1963.

balance of earning and non-earning investments, and long and short gestation projects. What is essential, however, is that a Plan should not be entered upon without any clear idea of where the finance is going to come from. It is consequently useful to draw up to start with an account of reliably available resources over the whole period. A sketch of such an account is shown in Table 5 (for

TABLE 5

PROSPECTIVE FINANCE FOR THE FIVE YEAR PLAN

Percentage distribution of estimated resources

1. *Local*
   a) Transfers from capital Fund   15
      (from revenue surpluses)
   b) Miscellaneous capital receipts   5
   c) Dividends from public enterprise   2
   d) Interest on loans, and repayments   5
   e) Borrowing from the Central Bank   13
   f) Local public issues   10
                                                          ___
                                                           50

2. *External*
   a) Grants from abroad   5
   b) Loans already arranged   20
   c) Loans being negotiated   15
                                                          ___
      Total prospective finance   90
      Gap to be financed from other sources   10
                                                          ___
                                                          100

simplicity of comparison it is shown only in percentage terms; for operational use it would naturally require to be in actual money terms). Such an account will be of great use to the government and its planners for internal purposes. It will also be a most valuable aid to potential lenders in judging the financial reliability of a would-be borrower. It is naturally not very likely that the financial resources which will be available over the whole plan period can be accurately foreseen from the start. Their relative order of magnitude should, however, be reasonably clear, so that the uncovered gap can be kept within reasonable dimensions of something like the 10 per cent. shown. How far such an account will be fulfilled as the Plan unrolls depends not only on the realisation of expectations, but also on the skill of administration and the control of outlay, subjects which we must now turn to consider.

Before leaving the subject of Plan organisation a remaining point should be made clear. The machinery we have sketched should not be regarded as a blue print for any country to adopt. Each country must think out the most appropriate machinery in the light of its own circumstances. The machinery will not be successful if it does not pay due attention to the relative roles of professional planners, political decisions and executive departments. Each succeeding step in the process of plan and implementation and of choice of the financial framework calls for separate and careful consideration.

CHAPTER EIGHT

BUDGETING AND THE
CONTROL OF EXPENDITURE

1. *The Purposes of the Budget*

IN the last chapter, when we were discussing the process of annual programming and adjustment of the Plan, it was suggested that this review should coincide with the preparation of the Budget Estimates. It was further suggested that both exercises should begin about half way through the financial year before the one to which they relate. There are several reasons why it is convenient to synchronise the discussions of total public outlay and its finance.

In the first place many projects in the Plan will probably be either extensions to existing installations or new installations similar to those already in operation. It is obviously desirable to review the whole of a service at once, including the condition and efficiency of existing equipment. Secondly, the time profile of Plan outlay is always uncertain. A serious divergence between projected and realised investment may require adjustment of existing services (for instance, the working of equipment more intensively in the short period to fill the gap until Plan outlay has caught up). Possibly the content of the Plan itself will have to be changed or rephased. Similar give and take between Budget and Plan is often required on the financial side also. Expected grants or loans turn out not to be available, or to be delayed; labour and materials tend to cost more when orders come to be given than they did when the Plan was drawn up. On each side of the account the Budget has, as best it can, to compensate for the vagaries of Plan execution.

Finally it is only by considering together the contractual obligations of continuing services and of Plan outlay that a correct estimate can be made of what is available for the Plan in the current Budget exercise. This is not to imply that Plan expenditure is to be regarded as a residual; what needs emphasis is that the joint review is partly an opportunity for seeing what economies can be made in existing current and maintenance expenditure so that as much room as possible can be found for development. This last process should properly be carried out against the background of the national accounts, and so include the legitimate expectations of the private sector. Once the point has been reached when estimates of National Income and Expenditure (or at least of the more important intersectoral flows) can be made regularly, it is convenient to have the annual national accounts prepared so as to coincide[1] with Budget finalisation and Plan review. The purpose of timing these reviews to commence about half way through the financial year is (as we saw in the last chapter) to ensure that they take place when experience of the current year's working has been gained. If detailed estimating takes place too early it may well be found when the Budget is completed that it is already out of date.

By the Budget is here meant the annual summary account of both the incomings and outgoings of the government, prepared by the Ministry of Finance (Treasury), or, if the Constitution does not provide for a Ministerial system, by an independent secretariat (such as the U.S. Bureau of the Budget), reporting directly to the Chief Executive. Although the Budget should not be the slave of annuality, in the sense that it must be accepted that expenditures and revenue collections are continuous processes, it is essential that there should be a thorough stocktaking of the financial and economic situation at not too distant intervals. The obvious choice for this is the physical year, to which everything else fundamentally conforms. Consistent with this annuality, however, there is a considerable range of choice open for the dating of the accounting year and consequently for the budget debates. The choice should be made primarily on climatic and local economic grounds; it is too often fixed by historical accident or blind following of precedent.

Properly understood the Budget is both a backward and a forward looking account. Looking backward the last available Actuals should be set against their Estimates. Every effort should be made to have the former as recent as possible, for preference referring to the year just ending, so that they are fully up to date. In the U.K. this is achieved by a system of a weekly account of issues from the Exchequer. At the end of the financial year all books are closed and any bills which have not been paid are excluded. The

---

1. In the U.K. this is brought about by making up the national accounts to the calendar year (this is more convenient for information from the private sector also), and the budget accounts for the financial year (April to March). The most up to date information on the national accounts is consequently available from December when the Treasury finally reviews the Estimates.

weekly record (together with the self-accounting system presently to be described) makes it unlikely that payments will be deliberately held back in order to improve the appearance of the departmental accounts. Naturally figures of disbursements issued so close to the end of the financial year do not permit of a detailed economic breakdown; but this can come later. At the moment it is the total that matters most. It is essential to the system that any balances in departments at the end of the year should (notionally) be handed back to the Exchequer, so that each budget exercise is, in an important sense, self contained.

The Budget is the main opportunity for examining all the economic aspects of the country's position. Consequently to bring out its full significance the Budget needs to be accompanied by as much supplementary information as possible. For very important services such as defence it is useful to have a separate sub-budget, so that a full breakdown of the figures is available during the debates. The preliminary national accounts, including the account of the balance of payments, should ideally also be available. There will also be the annual Report on Plan progress to be considered. Finally for a considered appreciation of the economic situation a detailed Memorandum prepared in the Ministry of Finance should be issued with the figures. Apart from the figures themselves this is the most important item; on the skill with which it is drawn up the government's success or failure in carrying out its policy will largely turn.

The Budget account has to serve a number of different purposes, so that whatever the form in which it is presented it is inevitably something of a compromise. The first purpose of the expenditure account is to record disbursements and to provide explanations of any discrepancies from the Estimates which may have occurred in the course of the year's working. This is, so far as the ordinary administrative services are concerned, mainly a check on accuracy and honesty. The importance of service reliability cannot be too much stressed in the early stages of development (especially where independence has only recently been achieved). Corruption is bad in any place and time, but for a country trying desperately to get ahead with slender resources, inability to rely on the accuracy of administration largely frustrates the efforts of its rulers and planners. Accuracy is equally necessary from the planning point of view. It is impossible to build a sensible policy on the quick-sands of misrepresentation. So far as development expenditure is concerned the check on the Estimates is inevitably less exact than that of normal services, because of the uncertainty of the rate of investment. But as we have seen, there is much that can be done to increase precision by careful phasing against a background of expected time profiles, based on experience of similar works.

The second purpose of the budget account is to display—to the Cabinet, the Legislature, the press and the public—the proposed lay-out of expenditure and the suggested means of financing it. The account must be the basis for an informed judgment on the first two levels of choice (see chapter 2): the relation between the public and the private sector's respective command over resources and the distribution of the public sector's share over different services. The basis of the first choice is (as we have seen) the opportunity cost of foregoing alternative uses of the resources, broadly represented by the taxes which need to be raised to finance the public share. This is not, as we know, merely a question of the size of the total tax bill, but is intimately related to the choice of taxes both from the distributional and from the incentive points of view.

Thirdly, in conjunction with the national accounts, the influence of the public sector in the economy should be made plain in the Budget. This is important because public expenditure has very different multiplier and accelerator effects from private spending. This difference is obvious in respect of redistributive transfers; it is no less important on capital account. New obligations are created by public investment most of which are not self-sustaining. On the other side a greatly intensified demand for certain economic resources is set up, largely in the constructional trades and heavy industries (and hence for imports). Finally, as the central record of the government's activities, the Budget is the great opportunity to demonstrate to the world (and especially to potential lenders) that the country is efficiently run and that its finances are soundly under control. The form of budget account should be chosen so that it will show this clearly.

2. *Simplicity and Comprehensiveness*

To fulfill all these purposes the budget account must display two characteristics: it must be simple and it must be comprehensive. Neither of these is easy to achieve. Simplicity is essential in order that the wood can be seen and appreciated, unencumbered by a rank growth of trees. Even with a clear Economic Memorandum

it is all too easy—for both legislators and the public—to concentrate their attention on particular trees, which then assume
undue prominence. Probably this is inevitable, and up to a point
not undesirable, since debates on expenditure (in Committee of
Supply) are a unique opportunity for general criticism and the
ventilation of grievances; but there is no excuse for the use of a
form of account which exaggerates the parts at the expense of the
whole. The need for simplicity is to some extent in conflict with
the somewhat considerable detail that is essential for an accuracy
check. It is, however, probably true that in all countries budget
accounts will take substantial streamlining without the loss of
essential detail.[1] Further, as administrative expertise and reliability increases it becomes progressively possible to reduce
detailed control and at the same time to increase flexibility, by
voting expenditure in large blocks.[2]

Comprehensiveness is essential in order to display the true
balance between revenue and expenditure. A first step to achieving
comprehensiveness is to ensure that all incomings, whether from
taxes or other sources, are paid into a single Consolidated Fund,
and that all issues for disbursement are made from this Fund. It is
essential that the Fund should be inviolable and that issues from it
are sanctioned by a single officer of outstanding and independent
status. Comprehensiveness implies that the net results (after providing for capital consumption and debt service) of public trading
and manufacturing activities and of 'self-balancing' accounts
should be brought into the budget. The commercial accounts of
the undertakings should, however, also be available at the time of
the debates. Clarity will be enhanced if so far as possible the
Estimates are arranged on a functional basis (so that it is possible
to discern their economic significance at a glance), rather than
according to the traditional classification by inputs (so much for
wages and salaries, telephone calls, purchase of materials, and so on
over a whole Ministry or Service). The input classification is only
useful for a crude accuracy check.

1. The British Treasury recently came to the conclusion that it could cut
down the Estimates from 1200 to 430 pages without a serious loss of information.
Additional detail on any point would be supplied on demand. cf. U. K. Hicks,
'Plowden, Planning and Control', Public Administration, Winter 1961.
2. Thus the whole of expenditure on hospitals under the British National
Health Service is now put into one 'Vote'; this does not prevent any individual
point being raised in Committee of Supply, but it does mean that the detailed
application of funds can be settled autonomously within the Service.

While in a sense the preparation of the Estimates must be a continuous process as expenditure takes place—the lessons of one year need to be carried forward to the next—the formal work of drawing up the Estimates is better done as rapidly as possible (subject to the job not being scamped), so that they are as up to date as possible when they come to be debated. The first work on the Estimates must of necessity be carried out within the spending departments. (It is convenient for them at this stage to work to 'notional' totals, as was suggested for Plan Estimates.) But it is for the Ministry of Finance to examine the drafts in detail, questioning and pruning where necessary, and above all not taking the easy way out of accepting a figure that is no different from last year's, unless it can be shown to be right for this year. If it carries out this process intelligently the Ministry of Finance will find that as a by-product it will have acquired the grasp of the situation which it will need for determining the final make up of the Budget.

3. *The Estimates, the Consolidated Fund and the Civil Contingencies Fund*

Discussion of the Estimates in the Legislature needs to be long enough for considered debate,[1] and, as the House will have other current business which cannot be neglected, this means that the whole process of budgetary debate will occupy perhaps several months. On the other hand the discussion must not be so long drawn out as to delay Appropriation for more than a few months (three to four) of the financial year to which they relate. Over a period of this length it is quite feasible to carry on the finance of services by means of Votes on Account which will be well within the Budgetary provision. To attempt to do so for a much longer period risks expenditure getting out of hand and disrupting the Budget frame. There are substantial arguments in favour of conducting the debates 'on the floor of the House' in 'Committee of the Whole', since all members are then given the fullest opportunity to co-operate throughout the process. Under the alternative Select Committee procedure those Members who are not on the Committee can of necessity only be given a very hurried

---

1. Before independence it was the British colonial practice to use debates in the 'Legislative Council' only to serve as an opportunity for the airing of grievances, the real business being transacted in the Executive Council. Consequently only a very short time was allowed—in India fourteen days.

opportunity of co-operation or the whole process would become intolerably drawn out.

Whatever method is used it is wise to put a definite time limit to the discussion of the Estimates, since there is no natural limit to the subjects which might plausibly be discussed. There are two devices here which have been taken over from the British Parliament in a number of countries. First, it is virtually essential to have a Standing Order making it impossible for any Member of the Legislature who is not a Member of the government to introduce an amendment which would require additional finance if adopted.[1] This effectively prevents the Budget structure from being inflated or seriously distorted. Secondly, if some of the Votes have not been passed by the time the time limit arrives the debates themselves can be forced into a procrustean bed by some form of Closure order. This is by no means an ideal solution; but it may well be preferable to the alternative of failing to pass the Budget within the allotted time.

If the Estimates of outlay are debated in Committee of the Whole it is natural that the Incomings side of the Budget should be similarly treated. Since taxes are a somewhat technical matter there is usually less trouble—or interest—in respect of the debates on this side of the account. It is vitally important that the tax Committee (usually known as Ways and Means) should work to a single Finance Act, the counterpart of the single Appropriation Act embodying the Estimates. This can easily be achieved by putting all fiscal matters and all tax changes into a single Finance Bill, and arranging that this must be passed by the date fixed for the Estimates. The sanction for this is for the appropriate officer[2] to refuse a further Vote on Account until the Bill is passed. The Financial Statement concerning Incomings which should accompany the introduction to the Legislature of the complete Budget account should also show the estimated revenue effect of proposed changes in the tax system. To prevent forestalling in the attempt

1. In drawing up the Constitution for Western Germany at the end of World War Two the Allies (U.S. and U.K.) attempted a compromise on this point by writing in a provision that if a Member proposed an amendment which involved additional finance he must also propose the means to raise it. This proved completely abortive since there is nothing to prevent the tax proposals from being frivolous and irrelevant.

2. In the U.K. this is the Comptroller and Auditor General who is in charge of the Consolidated Fund. The sanction has only once been invoked—significantly on the occasion of the first step towards the welfare state: the introduction of progressive supertax to finance social security.

to evade the effects of expected tax changes it is wise to pass all changes provisionally into law on the same day as they are announced. If later the changes are not fully accepted by the House tax can be refunded where it has been overpaid.

It will be apparent from this discussion that orderly budgeting requires that all government outgoings and incomings should be kept within a single account. This is the true meaning of comprehensiveness. In principle Actuals will then exactly mirror Estimates and any divergences be immediately apparent.[1] There are, however, at least three reasons why in the modern world this ideal can no longer be realised completely. This is not a matter of any difference between advanced and development countries; it is due to the expanded commitments of modern public sectors, entailing (even apart from Plan outlay) for certain services precise commitments which cannot be foreseen in advance. 'Open ended' commitments are of increasing range and importance. One source of these indeed is by no means new: national debt service, especially on short term obligations. A change in borrowing rates on this count may make a not inconsiderable difference to budgetary outlay. Formerly short term obligations formed a much smaller proportion of total debt than has now become usual. On the other hand the governments of those days had no means whatever of controlling short term interest rates. In many countries today they are to a very considerable extent within the control of the monetary authorities. Development countries can hope to approach this position progressively as their central banks find their feet. It would not be desirable, however, to control interest rates too exclusively in the interests of the budget. Countries where interest rates are not yet within the control of the authorities will be wise to exercise discretion in borrowing on short term, especially for long term investment.

Generally speaking the more highly the social services are developed the greater the volume of open ended commitments. These may arise in several ways: for instance through grants to persons for medical attention, or to lower layer governments who have been guaranteed assistance when they open new schools, train additional teachers or undertake other specific types of works. Another source of open ended expenditure is the guarantee to provide assistance for local calamities such as drought or flood (relief

1. cf. J. R. Hicks, *The Problem of Budgetary Reform*, Oxford, 1949, and U. K. Hicks, 'The Control of Public Expenditure', *Lloyds Bank Review*, April 1961.

of calamities on a national scale such as hurricane, earthquake or volcanic erruption cannot be provided within the Budget). The fact that many of these outlays are unpredictable does not, however, exonerate the budget planners from making the best forecast of their incidence that they can.

A very general type of expenditure which cannot be precisely budgeted for is the rising cost of wages and salaries in the public services. One aspect of this, normal 'creep' due to increasing years of service, can indeed be accurately estimated, so long as records of contracts are kept; but the element due to wage and salary increases, which in most development countries are now negotiated on a national scale, cannot be allowed for in the same way. There are two possible budgetary procedures. One is to include an allowance to cover pay rates which have been agreed although they have not yet come into force. The economic effects of public expenditure can probably be judged more accurately along this line than along the alternative which pays no attention to rates of pay that are not actually in force at the time the Budget is drawn up. From the point of view of close budgeting, however, the latter is unquestionably the better alternative. It is parallel to the normal exclusion of expenditures which have not actually been made at the time the accounts are closed. Naturally, however, in planning the economically correct surplus to aim for, these matters will be borne in mind.

Finally, there is an awkward problem concerned with what may be called the 'setting up' costs of new services, for example a pensions scheme, or changes in state or local authority boundaries calling for new offices. Before actual proposals can sensibly be put before the Legislature a number of preliminary expenses have to be incurred: an estimate needs to be made of the extent of demand —the population to be served.[1] This must be followed up by a weighing up of establishment costs: estimates of numbers of different grades of clerical and administrative staff and their proposed location (since this may affect their cost). Moreover their grading has to be fitted in with the pay and conditions of personnel in similar grades in occupations already established. Further, estimates need to be made of the availability of the different grades which will be required, and consequently for the need and type of

1. It may be desirable to distinguish between short and long period demand. When the British National Health Service was established there was an explosion of demand for such amenities as spectacles and dentures. It was several years before the backlog demand was satisfied and a normal outlay could be forecast.

training called for.[1] Finally estimates are required of the cost of buildings and lánd acquisition at the points where the service will be carried on.

On the planning side the carrying out of these preliminaries is not much different from that of any other planning exercise; the basic difference, however, is that final decisions have not yet been taken in respect of the new service, and in fact to a large extent depend on the results of these preliminary exercises. They are, however, a once for all operation. Hence it is desirable to find a means of financing them which is outside the Estimates, but not altogether outside the control of the Legislature. For all such purposes it is convenient to establish a Civil Contingencies Fund. The Legislature sanctions the total amount of this. Advances for such purposes as we have been describing must be repaid to the Fund by the end of the financial year, if necessary by raising additional tax revenue. The Legislature can, however, from time to time vote additional moneys for the Fund, according to the needs to be met.

4. *Choice of Budgetary Form*

So far we have not discussed in detail the form of the Budget. Until recently the forms used reflected only needs of administrative convenience and in some cases reliability control. In Continental countries it has long been customary to present an 'ordinary' and an 'extraordinary' budget, the former alone being covered by current revenue. Without a careful definition of either what was to be regarded as 'current revenue' or of what types of expenditure should be covered by it, all significance of the difference between the two accounts was lost, and slack taxation very naturally followed.

The British tradition, thanks to the tight practices established by Gladstone in the 1860's and 70's, evolved in a somewhat different manner. In the Budget proper there appeared only current outlay (public consumption) and current receipts, geared strictly to balance, including some surplus for the repayment of debt. No borrowing took place except for wars. All defence equipment was written down to zero value immediately and so was counted as current consumption. The loans out of which some of it at least would have been financed could not, however, be regarded as current incomings. They had no assets standing against them (or rather they had already been written down to zero value). Con-

1. cf. Report of the Civil Service Commission for the Eastern Caribbean, Cmd. 1992 of 1963.

sequently incomings from the loans could not figure in the Budget proper; but for the sake of completeness a line was drawn and they were set out below. As time went on the government began to raise loans to acquire assets such as the shares of the Suez canal, and during the First World War some Australian mineral interests. These loans bore interest and it was anticipated that in due course they would be repaid. They were clearly in a different class from those representing 'dead weight' (or non-asset) debt. Yet they had no more right to appear in the Budget, and consequently all such transactions were also entered 'below the line'.

More recently, and especially after the Second World War, the government rapidly expanded its financial transactions of a commercial or semi-commercial nature. Loans were made to such organisations as the Coal Board (and later to other nationalised industries), to the Post Office and to local authorities for capital works. The government even indulged in some direct capital formation itself, mainly for housing. Thus the below the line account gradually expanded until it would have resembled a true capital account, had it been organised with any economic significance. This stage was, however, temporary; in the years following the war the government gradually shed its commercial responsibilities or decided to organise them as separate public corporations. One of the most recent to undergo this change was the Post Office.

Hence the government's transactions on capital account have come to be almost wholly financial transactions. By this time the technique of social accounting had been fully developed and the Central Statistical Office was publishing regularly, year by year, not only the national accounts with a full record of intersectoral flows, but also complete current and capital accounts of the central government and of the other parts of the public sector. The planners were thus provided with all the available information outside the budget accounts. In view of the objective of presenting a simple budget account as well as the desirability of continuity, it was consequently decided wholly to abandon a capital account, to abolish 'the line' and to show all government expenditure in a single account.[1]

1. There has been proposed, however, to set up an additional Finance Account recording all purely financial transactions of the government, including such things as subscriptions to the World Bank and International Monetary Fund. For further information on all this see Reform of the Exchequer Accounts, Cmd 2014 of 1963, and comment by J. R. and U. K. Hicks in *Bulletin of the Oxford Institute of Economics and Statistics*, 1963.

It must be observed that in the U.K. it is only the existence of regular issues of the complete national accounts with an adequate current and capital breakdown of the public sector (as well as summary commercial accounts of nationalised industries and other government commercial interests) that makes a simplified Budget of this type adequate for planning and policy decisions. In a development country the situation is very different. Even if national income and expenditure is regularly calculated there are a number of reasons (several of which we have examined) why the account may not give a sufficiently firm breakdown of current and capital items. For any country that takes its planning seriously it is essential that a properly organised current and capital account should be available, on which plans and decisions will be based. It is probable that this will have to be provided in the Budget. Indeed, for a development country it is a positive advantage to have the economic and fiscal breakdown in a single account, for the information both of the home public and of potential lenders abroad. The central government Budget[1] consequently needs to be drawn up in a fully developed current and capital form. Table 6 illustrates a normal arrangement of this. It differs from the internationally agreed form only in giving rather more detail of the results of government commercial activities and in making explicit provision for capital consumption (replacement) in non or para-trading services, to allow for the large part such services play in the early stages of development.

This is a strictly summary account. Nevertheless the basic distinctions between transfers and true income and between transfer expenditure and purchases of goods and services· are carefully drawn. This is necessary for an appreciation of the effects of the Budget, because of their different (control or expansionary) effects and the distributional changes thereby implied. On the outgoings side the details of supply expenditure should already be familiar from the Estimates, but it is as well to repeat the main headings. In a parallel manner collections under the different tax headings should be distinguished. In respect of transfers on the outgoings side there may well be a number of 'empty boxes' since (as we have seen) social transfers occupy a much less important place in a development than in an advanced country.

---

1. The same holds for state or regional budgets in a federation, and so far as possible for local authorities.

Two small deviations from established practice require a word of justification. The object of entering surpluses and deficits on self balancing and commercial accounts separately is to ensure a better record of the results. A footnote will list which are the activities on which they have respectively been realised. It is advisable only to record a surplus after due provision has been made for capital consumption and debt service. If a deficit has been so serious as not to cover these charges it should be specially noted. It is very common experience (but bad policy) to find that 'self balancing' services do not, in fact, balance, so that uncovered costs have to be met from general taxation. This probably falls partly on those who do not have access to the services, a manifestly unfair imposition.

The provision (item 3 on the outgoings side) for capital consumption is intended to refer to non-trading or non-self-balancing services. Since for these there are no incomings which can be applied to this purpose it is unavoidable to provide for depreciation in some other way. The usual (but by no means universal) practice in public management is to raise a new loan when installations have to be replaced. In a development country, however, there are two cogent reasons which point to the desirability of making current provision for replacement out of taxation. In the first place, since loans are not easy to raise they are better reserved for new works. Secondly, it is almost certain that the works (schools, hospitals and so on) will be better looked after if there is a periodical reminder that forward commitments are accumulating. The period over which the installations should be written off in this way depends mainly on the physical life of the equipment, obsolescence being a less important consideration than in respect of commercial undertakings. The object of distinguishing new from existing works is to give an opportunity for estimating the normal rate of physical capital consumption (since no two works are exactly similar) as experience of working is gained.

The key figure in the whole budget account is the surplus (or deficit) on the current account. This registers the contribution of the government to national saving (or dissaving), and is a measure of great economic significance. Unless after due forethought and circumspection it has been decided that in this particular year there should be a controlled dose of deficit finance, the current budget should show a positive balance. Indeed, in view of the expansionary nature of the development process it is generally

6. THE GENERAL BUDGET

Incomings	Outgoings

I. CURRENT (REVENUE) ACCOUNT

1. *By Transfers*
  a. Tax revenue[1]
  b. Licenses
  c. Royalties
  d. From abroad (grants)
 	
2. *By True Income*
  a. Fees, fines, penalties, etc.
  b. Rent and Interest
  c. Surplus on self-balancing
    A/Cs
  d. Surplus on public enterprises
	1. *On Goods and Services*
	  a. Supply[2]
	  b. Defence
	  c. Tax collection
	
	2. *On Transfers*
	  a. National Debt Interest
	  b. Grants to Persons
	    (including subsidies)[3]
	  c. Grants to local authorities
	  d. Grants to private bodies:
	    i. Charities, etc.
	    ii. Firms
	  e. Deficits on self-balancing
	    A/Cs
	  f. Deficits on public
	    enterprises
	3. *Provision for capital consumption*
	  a. Existing works
	  b. New works (up to 5 years)

Incomings (1 + 2) Less Outgoings (1 + 2 + 3) = net current surplus/ deficit

1. Main heads should be distinguished: i.e. Income Tax, Company Tax, Export Taxes, Import Duties, Excises, etc.
2. Main Heads should be distinguished, i.e. Administration, Defence, Overseas Representation, etc., Communications, Education, Health, Welfare, Agriculture and Industry current services.
3. i.e. income subsidies (grants to persons) and outlay subsidies which enable goods to be purchased below cost.

II. CAPITAL (INVESTMENT) ACCOUNT

1. *From Current Budget*
  a. Capital Consumption
  b. Net Current Surplus
 	
2. *Sales of Government Property*
	1. *Real Investment*
	  a. Maintenance/Replacement
	  b. New Construction
	  c. Value of changes in stores
	    etc.

II. Capital (Investment) Account—*(continued)*

3. *Loan Repayments (to)*
   a. at home
   b. abroad

4. *New Loans Raised*
   a. at home
   b. abroad

5. *Capital Grants from abroad*

2. *Purchase of assets from private sector*

3. *Loan repayments (by)*
   a. at home
   b. abroad

4. *New Lending & Advances*
   a. Civil Contingencies Fund
   b. Transport corporations
   c. Fuel & Power Corporations
   d. Communications & Broadcasting
   e. I.D.C. A.D.C. etc.
   f. Local Authorities
   g. Other

5. *Capital Grants*
   a. Local Authorities
   b. Private sector

Incomings $(1 + 2 + 3 + 4 + 5)$ *Less* Outgoings $(1 + 2 + 3 + 4 + 5)$ = Change in accumulated balances (liquidity)

---

desirable that there should be a sufficient surplus of current incomings to finance some new investment as well as replacement.

The first item on the incomings side of the capital (or investment) account is accordingly the gross surplus from the current budget. (Had it been a deficit it would naturally figure on the outgoings side.) The other items on the incomings side record the means of financing investment, other than any self financing which commercial undertakings may be able to provide out of their profits. (The record of this will be found in their commercial accounts.) It may not always be clear whether grants from abroad belong properly to current or capital account. Generally speaking it is better to keep them out of the current account unless they are part of a regular series, such as a former colonial power might continue to give after independence.

It will be seen that the outgoings side of the investment account comprises two different types of transaction: real investment, covering gross fixed capital formation and stock changes, and financial transactions. Purchase of assets from the private sector is most likely to be concerned with land acquisition; it might, however, include such things as purchase of shares in private companies or compensation for nationalisation. The remaining outgoings consist of capital transfers, of which we can distinguish five types: (i) advances to the Civil Contingencies Fund if it requires strengthening; (ii) loans and advances to public corporations engaged in operating utilities, building roads and so on; (iii) advances to such bodies as the Industrial Development and Agricultural Development Corporations (in so far as they do not obtain their funds direct from the Central Bank); (iv) loans to local authorities (or in a federation to states); (v) to the private sector either in the form of economic aid to firms or for social purposes (such as to Mission or other charitable schools). Sufficient information to identify the relative importance of these purposes should naturally be provided in the account.

It may be convenient to aid lower layer governments by grants rather than by loans. This has the advantage not only of leaving no aftermath of debt service, but also of giving the higher layer government more control over the disposal of the funds (as we discussed in Chapter VI). A careful record of both loans and grants has the advantage, in addition to completing the national government account, of providing a pointer to the investment the grant receiving bodies are likely to undertake, in advance of direct information which may later be received from them, and so will be of assistance to the planners. The final balance of the entire Budget is a figure of considerable economic significance, although not so great as that of the outcome of the current account. It registers the change in the accumulated balances of the government and hence of its liquidity. While a country is in the active stage of a development process it cannot be expected that the total budget will show a surplus; but if due provision is being made for debt service this need cause no apprehension.

5. *The Administration of Expenditure Control*

The outgoings side of the Budget is, as we have seen, the government's plan for the allocation of funds—and hence of the real resources over which it has control. Once the implementation of the Estimates has begun the machinery for the control of expenditure must come into play. This is not a simple exercise and is best approached from several angles, since there are a number of objectives to be served. The first necessity is to see that expenditure is being made only for the purposes[1] and so far as possible only in the amounts stated and agreed in the Estimates; and secondly when the year's spending has been completed, to check by means of Audit that this result has been achieved—or if it has not, to discover why. These accuracy checks are only the beginning of expenditure control; it is equally necessary to evaluate the efficiency of the administration and execution of public outlay. For both types of check it is (as we shall see) useful to enlist the co-operation of Members of the Legislature in Select Committee. This ensures that some members will have inside knowledge of some of the details of expenditure, which they can communicate directly to their colleagues. Moreover committee work is extremely educative for the Members themselves. In particular it has proved an excellent way of inculcating a spirit of constructive and responsible criticism among members of the Opposition.

The control of public expenditure necessarily starts in the spending Ministries, as outlay takes place. Broadly there are two alternative methods in use, known respectively as the Pre-audit and the Self-accounting system. The first is the more appropriate where administrators are inexperienced and perhaps subject to strong external pressures. In this system all disbursements must be certified in advance by an officer known as the Accountant General. When it is conscientiously operated this system seems to be completely effective in preventing irregularities.[2] It may, however, entail frustrating delays, especially where the lines of communication are long. In a large country where delay occurs it can be mitigated by appointing sub-offices for pre-audit in different places; but this risks some loss of control. In the pre-audit system very much depends on the integrity of the Accountant General and

1. This does not imply that *virement*, or the transfer of funds voted for one purpose to another use, must never take place, a condition that would impose far too great a degree of rigidity. But it does imply that *virement* should be strictly limited and subject to the permission of the Ministry of Finance. With modern communications even in most development countries there is now no excuse for the easy terms of *virement* which have long been in operation. As we have seen, when responsibility can be taken for granted any desired degree of flexibility can be obtained by enlarging the size of the Votes (blocks) in which the Estimates are appropriated.

2. cf. Report of the Fiscal Commissioner in the Eastern Caribbean, cit., on the difference between Barbados and some of the other islands.

the skill with which he organises his office. An alternative device, which has been tried extensively in the U.S.A., is to restrict Departments to a monthly ration of funds. Since by no means all expenditure takes place at a regular rate this device also suffers from uncomfortable rigidity.

Under the self-accounting system the personal responsibility for orderly disbursements rests on the Head of Department (the Permanent Secretary) who is also the Accounting Officer. When the Appropriation Act is passed the Accounting Officer effectively opens an account for his Ministry with the Consolidated Fund. He can draw on this as required for the purposes of the Department, simply by communicating with the Paymaster General.[1] It is the personal responsibility of the Accounting Officer to see that disbursements take place only as directed, and that there is no overdrawing. Unspent balances must (as we have seen) notionally be returned at the end of the financial year.

The self-accounting system is obviously much more flexible than the pre-audit system. Expenditures can be made exactly when and as they are wanted. It presupposes, however, the existence of two conditions: firstly an Accounting Officer who is really in a position to control the spending of his Department, and secondly some sort of running audit, so that a close watch is kept on the rate of disbursement. In addition to the officers of the Department whose especial care this will be, it is useful to have some officers from the Department of Audit to work alongside them. They will help the spending Department to run straight; and when the closed accounts come to be audited they will have inside knowledge of the situations to which they refer.

A word may here be said on the control of expenditure where bulk orders for fixed or working capital are given to the private sector. This is a problem which concerns both Plan and routine expenditure, since contracts may be for regular supplies—for instance for schools or hospitals, or for stationery for government Departments—as well as in connection with the erection of specific works. In development countries there are few subjects which give rise to more trouble than the award of contracts (trouble is not by any means unknown in advanced countries also). No doubt part of the trouble is due to the fact that relatively big money is involved.

---

1. The Paymaster General's office under this system is merely a go-between. The authorising authority is the Comptroller and Auditor General, see above p. 163 and below p. 178.

This leads both members of the Legislature and civil servants to take an unhealthy interest in the subject; moreover it is one in which malversation is particularly easy. But there are also inherent difficulties.

It is customary to make statutory provision to prevent members of the Legislature or civil service from having any direct interest in the award of a contract; but this is only the beginning of a solution. There appear to be two problems in particular. First there is a strong and well recognised case for accepting always the lowest tender. This may, however, lead to trouble if the contractor has not, in fact, either the capital or the experience to carry through the job satisfactorily. Some flexibility must consequently be worked into the machinery; but it should be exercised by an independent Authority and not be at the discretion of the Ministry concerned. Secondly, it is vexatious and almost certainly unnecessary to put very small orders out to tender; it is sensible to draw a line below which a Ministry can use its discretion in ordering. But if the legislature is persuaded to raise the line substantially (as may on occasion happen)[1] there is grave danger of complete loss of control.

Against both of these troubles it is an obvious precaution to appoint independent Tenders Boards; but here again problems arise. If the jurisdiction of the Board is made too small it will be subject to all the pressures that beset direct contracting. If it is too large it runs the danger of being too remote to comprehend fully the real requirements of the situation. Some of the most difficult problems of contracting occur within the jurisdictions of lower layer governments, and here the central Plan organisation or the Ministry concerned may be able to exercise a guiding hand. There is no easy solution to the problems of contracting, but since contracts are such an important part of the development process it is worth making every effort to make sure they are satisfactory.

It is implicit in the budgetary system just described that for administrative Departments simple cash accounting is the only possible method; in no other way can the correspondence between Estimates and Actuals be preserved. This does not imply that the Estimates must continue to be arranged on an 'input' basis; on the contrary, so far as possible they should be functionally arranged so that it is possible to evaluate the true costs of a certain institution

---

1. This happened in the island of Grenada in 1961, bringing the accounts to the verge of bankruptcy: cf. Report of the Administrator (J. Lloyd).

or unit of service.[1] Only thus can efficiency in different units be compared. It may be necessary however for the sake of continuity in the accuracy check to set out a simple reconciliation account arranged by inputs in the traditional way.

At the other extreme it is quite essential that economic Departments, which for this purpose we may define as those operating with capital assets which they have a duty to maintain, should use a form of accounts which will show the results of their operations, their allocation to current and capital needs, and (where relevant) to taxation or to the general revenue appropriation account. For public corporations concerned with manufacturing or the provision of services such a business-type form of accounts is the natural one to adopt. Any government departments which are engaged in operations of this type are best hived off completely from the administrative accounting system. A problem arises, however, in respect of agencies which are not actually engaged in commercial activities but which are much concerned with capital assets such as the Roads Department or Office of Works (P.W.D.). It may not be possible to set up a complete commercial accounting system for these, yet it is obvious that a purely cash account will give a very inadequate record of their activities. Another difficulty is that the extent of their investment from year to year may vary very substantially, not due to commercial considerations but to the exigencies of the budgetary situation, to which they will be much more subject than will a true trading Department. The best solution seems to be to use a modified form of trading account, such as that shown below for a Roads Department.[2] From such an account the extent to which the road system is being improved, maintained or is deteriorating is at once apparent.

For all Departments, whether conducted on the pre-audit or self-accounting system, whatever their duties and whatever form

1. cf. Plowden Report on Control of Expenditure, cit.
2. cf. J. R. Hicks, *the Problem of Budgetary Reform:* (Oxford, 1948)
   Accounts of a Roads Department considered as a Trading Department

1. *Revenue Account*	C	Maintenance due	A
(Subsidy, Grant or earmarked tax)		Interest on government advances	b
		Surplus of profit $C-(A+b)$	

2. *Capital Account*			
Surplus of Profit	$C-(A+b)$	Gross Real Investment	d
Depreciation ($=A$)	D	Repayment of Advances	c
New government advances	F	Increase in cash	$(C+D+F)-$ $(A+b+d+c)$

of accounting proves to be the most appropriate, the final process of post-audit is vital, since it is only at this stage that it can really be ascertained what has been spent on different purposes. From the importance of the audit function it follows that the Auditor General must be an officer of very high standing and prestige. It is usual to give him the status and pay of a judge, so that he stands above party politics and can only be removed from his office for grave dereliction of duty and by the vote of both Houses of the Legislature (in a bi-cameral system).

If it is politically feasible for the central Audit Department to undertake also the audit of state (in a federation) and the larger local authority expenditure (as is done in India), this not only contributes to more accurate accounting throughout the public sector, but will also usefully increase the central government's knowledge of the efficiency (or otherwise) of lower layer governments. In many ways the most important aspect of the process of Audit is the detailed Report which the Auditor General should present and in which he will record his judgement of the performance of different Departments, and in particular draw attention to any misdemeanours. This Report can also be the basis for a further type of control, as we shall now discuss.

6. *Financial Select Committees of the Legislature*

So far we have been concerned only with expenditure control at the administrative level. It was hinted earlier, however, that Members of the Legislature can also be usefully brought into the process. The Report of the Auditor General can form the Agenda for examination by a Select Committee of the House on the Public Accounts. In the U.K. the P.A.C. was one of the Gladstone Reforms; the idea has been successfully transplanted to a number of Commonwealth countries, both advanced and developing. Some control by the Legislature will have already been exercised during the debates in Committee of Supply on the Estimates; but this is inevitably very general. The P.A.C. is very different. It acts as a tribunal, examining (on the suggestion of the Auditor General) the Accounting Officers of particular Departments. The examination is carried out in the presence of a representative of the Audit Department and one from the Ministry of Finance. For the Accounting Officer the examination may be extremely unpleasant; but there is no doubt that it operates as a strong deterrent to illegalities or even to carelessness in the disbursement of funds.

The P.A.C. is an extremely powerful instrument of control; it suffers, however, from the weakness that it can only function when the accounts are complete. This may easily be two years after the spending has taken place, by which time all public interest in it will probably have evaporated. Complementary Select Committees can, however, be set up to examine expenditure as it takes place. The Estimates Committee examines current expenditure as set out in the Estimates, either Department by Department or by function (which may straddle a number of Departments). Since the successful re-establishment of the Estimates Committee in the U.K. in 1946 it has made a number of important investigations and gained an enviable reputation for its success. The device has been copied with equal success in countries as diverse as India and Uganda. More recently a Select Committee on the Nationalised Industries has been set up in the U.K., so that for the first time the plans and accounts of these bodies can be brought under scrutiny. In a development country where such bodies are relatively more important a parallel committee could play a vital role. Without a special committee, however much it is suspected that money has been wasted (or worse) there may be no means of bringing the Management under examination.[1]

There are, however, two fundamental differences between these expenditure Committees and the Public Accounts Committee. In the first place they cannot have the prestige and authority of a tribunal because the budgetary exercise which they are examining is still incomplete. For a similar reason they must be careful in touching on policy decisions, since as Select Committees they must not appear to usurp the privilege of the whole House. Secondly, it follows from the fact that the accounts with which they are concerned are not yet complete that no authority can advise them on the investigations which they should make, in the way in which the Audit Department virtually writes the Agenda for the P.A.C. The expenditure committees must therefore rely on their own

---

1. For instance, let us say, a hotel has been built, partly by foreign loan, partly by home finance. The final cost turns out to be eight times as much as was estimated. What are the reasons? Only that part financed by loan from the government can normally come under the purview of the P.A.C. or the Estimates Committee, and this is quite insufficient to get to the bottom of the trouble.

perspicacity, backed up by suggestions from their own Secretariats[1] and perhaps from ideas gleaned from the press, to discover the most important matters to investigate. However active they may be there is no guarantee that they will cover the really important ones.

These three Select Committees (Public Accounts, Estimates and Nationalised Industries) will differ in detail according to the country in which they function. In the first place numbers will vary. In the U.K. the P.A.C. has traditionally had fifteen members; but the Estimates Committee is more than twice as large. (This is due to the fact that because of the wide and dispersed nature of its investigations it finds it convenient to operate a number of sub-committees who work on particular subjects and then report to the whole, before the Report is finalised and forwarded to the Department in question for comments.) Only fairly large legislatures can afford committees of these dimensions, for it is essential that members should not be so overburdened that they cannot attend properly to both their committee work and to other legislative duties. Small legislatures may not be able to spare members for more than one committee. In this case it is probably wise to concentrate on the Public Accounts Committee, partly because accuracy in spending is fundamental but also partly because they are the most appropriate body[2] for examining capital expenditure. Owing to the uncertain time profile of investment, examination during the course of implementation may be quite misleading.

In whatever ways the financial Select Committees may differ in practical details, or even in their coverage, there are certain principles which (experience shows) must be observed for them to be effective. The tradition whereby their respective party allegiance should mirror that of the House is important, and even more so is the tradition that Chairmen should always be members of the Opposition. If the weakness of the Opposition is such as to make this not feasible the chairman must be a man of strong personality and independent judgement, although a member of the party in

1. It is essential for the good working of the Committees that they should be adequately serviced; this was only gradually discovered in the U.K. See below for further discussion.

2. This has been demonstrated in respect of British Defence projects such as the Bloodhound missile contracted to Ferranti, in which the P.A.C. uncovered a most unfortunate situation (this had arisen fundamentally from the difficulty of forecasting research and development crests). cf. *The Times*, 23 April 1964.

power; this alternative has worked very well in India. The ideal is to have as chairman an experienced Member who held some financial or economic post when his party was in power. In many development countries, however, it will be some years before it is possible to realise this. The reasons for this insistence on an Opposition chairman are two. First, a chairman from the government party is likely to be too anxious to defend the policy of his party to make a sufficiently inquisitive chairman:[1] In quite a different context, the development of a constructive and informed Opposition is one of the great safeguards of the system of elective democracy. Responsibility, which carries with it some obligation to specialised work, is one of the best ways of ensuring this.

For the good working of the Financial Select Committees it is essential that they should be supported with adequate research and technical staff. In respect of the Public Accounts Committee this is less needed than for the others because they will have the help of the Audit Department. Nevertheless when they are investigating expenditure with economic implications (as may easily happen) they will be in urgent need of the help at least of the Statistical Office and its economists. The other two Committees will require both secretariat assistance and trained specialists on whom they can draw, almost all the time. This will be especially true in respect of the Nationalised Industries Committee, since many of their problems will be intricate and technical. This provision is essential if the reports of the Committees are to be authoritative; but it is probably not essential that all the staff should be engaged full time on their work.

The culmination of the investigations must be publication of the Reports, debate in the House and comment in the press.[2] Full publicity will enhance the understanding and responsibility of those Members of the House who are not members of the Committees as well as of those who are. It will contribute to the building up of 'an informed public opinion'[3] which is one of the most important safeguards of good democratic government.

It will be apparent from this discussion that controls adequate to ensure efficiency in the public services does not just happen; it calls for a continuing determination to make them work. The basic

1. This is exactly what happened in Canada.
2. The Reports of the U.K. Estimates Committee are published together with written replies from the Ministries which have been under fire.
3. cf. Plowden Committee, cit.

conditions for this are, on the part of Ministers, that they should devote their best ability to making informed policy decisions; they must seek and listen to expert advice, but at the same time they must keep their hands off the actual work of their Departments. On the side of the Departments it is essential for the government to be able to draw on a corps of dependable and trained career civil servants, not only in the higher 'decision making' ranks but right down through the clerical grades, who will work much more efficiently if they understand what they are doing and why it is to be done.[1]

A civil service of this calibre is not yet within the reach of all development countries; but a glance at those countries, such as India and Malaya, where it has already been obtained, will assuredly convince others of its importance. The basic answer is, of course, training. It would take us too far afield to discuss the various methods and opportunities of training now available to governments of development countries, both in advanced and in other development countries. Opportunities have recently very much improved. In particular, short courses for senior officers who cannot be released for a long period are available in a number of centres. For lower administrative and clerical grades help in establishing staff colleges can be obtained from the Technical Co-operation and Assistance Agencies.

Even well trained officers, however, cannot work well in bad conditions. Offices must be arranged with due attention to efficient organisation and management. An Organisation and Methods Department has long been established in the British Treasury, and no doubt in other countries, for the purpose of streamlining office organisation. In the U.K. it is said to have saved the Departments many thousands of pounds. Its services have been available on request to local authorities and to overseas governments. Recently, however, as a result of the investigations of the Plowden Committee, it has been concluded that by itself 'O & M' is not sufficient, and that the introduction of management techniques in the Departments (somewhat along the lines used widely in business in the U.S.A.) would ensure more efficient working at all levels. It has accordingly been decided to make provision in each Department for an additional high level officer whose special duty would be the management of the Department, thus setting free the Head of Department for more close attention to decision making, briefing

1. cf. Report of Fiscal Commission in the Eastern Caribbean.

of Ministers and attendance at conferences, duties which even in not very advanced development countries now occupy a great deal of his time.

A final necessity which is too often forgotten is that grade by grade, throughout the service, pay must be sufficient to ensure integrity and to provide incentive, through a regular system of in-service training and promotion. It will be the duty of whatever central Ministry is charged with Establishment (normally the Ministry of Finance) to see that everything is in order in this respect, as well as to attend to its multifarious other duties of finance and control. In this, as in other aspects of development, the way ahead is not easy, but a country which has a real will to develop will not hesitate to take it.

SOME USEFUL BOOKS

HAZLEWOOD A. D. (Ed.) *The Economics of 'Underdeveloped Areas', An Annotated Reading List*, Oxford, 2nd ed. 1959

HICKS, J. R. *The Social Framework*, 3rd Ed. Oxford, 1960

HICKS J. R. *Essays in World Economics*, Oxford, 1959

HICKS, U.K. *Public Finance*, Cambridge Economic Handbooks, Nisbet, 2nd ed. 1956

HICKS, U.K. *Development from Below*, Oxford, 1961

HICKS, U.K. *et al. Federation and Economic Growth*, Allen and Unwin, 1961

HIGGINS, B. H. *Economic Development*, Norton, New York, 1959

KALDOR, N. *Indian Tax Reform*, Government of India, 1957

KINDLEBERGER, C. P. *Economic Development*, Harvard Economics Handbooks, McGraw-Hill, New York, 1958

LEWIS, W. A. *The Theory of Economic Growth*, Allen and Unwin, 1959

MYINT, H. *The Economics of the Developing Countries*, Hutchinson 1964

NEVIN, E. T. *Capital Funds in Underdeveloped Countries*, Macmillan, 1961

PARANJAPE, H. K. *The (Indian) Planning Commission, A Descriptive Account*, Indian Institute of Public Administration, Delhi, 1964

PEACOCK AND ROBERTSON, ed. *Public Expenditure, Appraisal and Control*, Oliver and Boyd, Edinburgh, 1963

PREST, A. R. *Public Finance in Undeveloped Countries*, Weidenfeld and Nicolson, 1962

RICHARDSON, G. B. *Economic Theory*, Hutchinson, 1963

UNESCO, *Economic and Social Aspects of Educational Planning*, 1964

WALINSKY, L. J. *Planning and Execution of Economic Development*, McGraw-Hill, 1963

INDEX